Rapture

NO LIMITS

NO LIMITS

Edited by Costica Bradatan

The most important questions in life haunt us with a sense of boundlessness: there is no one right way to think about them or an exclusive place to look for answers. Philosophers and prophets, poets and scholars, scientists and artists—all are right in their quest for clarity and meaning. We care about these issues not simply in themselves but for ourselves—for us. To make sense of them is to understand who we are better. No Limits brings together creative thinkers who delight in the pleasure of intellectual hunting, wherever the hunt may take them and whatever critical boundaries they have to trample as they go. And in so doing they prove that such searching is not just rewarding but also transformative. There are no limits to knowledge and self-knowledge—just as there are none to self-fashioning.

Storythinking: The New Science of Narrative Intelligence, Angus
    Fletcher
Taste: A Book of Small Bites, Jehanne Dubrow
*Self-Improvement: Technologies of the Soul in the Age of Artificial
    Intelligence*, Mark Coeckelbergh
Inwardness: An Outsider's Guide, Jonardon Ganeri
Touch: Recovering Our Most Vital Sense, Richard Kearney
Intervolution: Smart Bodies Smart Things, Mark C. Taylor
Aimlessness, Tom Lutz

Rapture

Christopher Hamilton

Columbia University Press
New York

Columbia University Press
Publishers Since 1893
New York   Chichester, West Sussex
cup.columbia.edu

Library of Congress Cataloging-in-Publication Data
Names: Hamilton, Christopher, 1965– author.
Title: Rapture / Christopher Hamilton.
Description: New York : Columbia University Press, [2024] |
    Series: No limits | Includes bibliographical references and index.
Identifiers: LCCN 2023039217 (print) | LCCN 2023039218 (ebook) |
    ISBN 9780231201544 (hardback) | ISBN 9780231201551 (trade
    paperback) | ISBN 9780231561686 (ebook)
Subjects: LCSH: Rapture (Christian eschatology) | Self. | Religious
    awakening—Christianity.
Classification: LCC BT887 .H356 2024 (print) | LCC BT887 (ebook) |
    DDC 236—dc23/eng/20231106
LC record available at https://lccn.loc.gov/2023039217
LC ebook record available at https://lccn.loc.gov/2023039218

Cover design: Chang Jae Lee

For Nelly

We ought to dance with rapture that we should be alive and in the flesh, and part of the living, incarnate cosmos.

—D. H. LAWRENCE

Contents

Rapture

Introduction

Fragments of a Philosophy of Rapture

I suppose that it is, at least in part, a function of growing older that one feels this way, but it is hard to look at the world and not be overwhelmed by the sense of the endlessness of human folly, with all that entails by way of forms of violence, carelessness, and indifference. I mean: as one gets older, it becomes harder to retain the sense one had when one was younger that these things might someday be left behind, that human beings might grow up, come to their senses, and leave off living so negligently. And, of course, one sees so much folly in oneself, but the hope of youth that one might one day grow out of it all seems to recede into the distance as one gets older as just another expression of one's folly.

This sense of things coexists with another feature of human life, a feature to which Virginia Woolf draws attention. For most of life is lived in what Woolf called a kind of "non-being": "One walks, eats, sees things, deals with what has to be done; the broken vacuum cleaner; ordering dinner; writing orders to Mabel; washing; cooking dinner;

bookbinding."[1] Our lives are, for the most part, experienced, as Woolf indicates, as something extraordinarily flat, lacking anything much that carries us from one moment to the next other than a kind of inertia of a movement already started.

Given that our lives are like this, caught between a sense of the limitlessness of human folly, on the one hand, and the banality of our quotidian existence, on the other, philosophy really ought, in my view, to pay closer attention to those privileged moments that light up existence and give to it a kind of shape, form, or sense. Woolf called these "moments of being," moments when we see, as she puts it, behind or beyond the "cotton wool" of our lives and experience some kind of pattern or meaning. In this book, I think of moments of rapture as such moments and seek to explore them. And again my inspiration here is Woolf, who speaks, in her discussion of moments of being, of "the strongest pleasure known to me. It is the rapture I get when in writing I seem to be discovering what belongs to what; making a scene come right; making a character come together."[2]

There are, as Woolf's example helps to make clear, many ways in which one might think of moments of rapture, since one might not, I suppose, have thought that writing might provide one example of this. Be that as it may, to my mind, the paradigm case of rapture is the act of sexual love. Obviously enough, the intense pleasure that sex offers is central here: "erotic enjoyment is," as Christopher Ricks puts it in describing Keats's view, "the peak and crown of all pleasures."[3] But this is partly and importantly so, I think, because sex takes us in two directions at once: it offers a kind of release from the self, the experience of being beyond or outside oneself, combined with a return to the self, an increased sense of oneself. In sex, one loses oneself and yet finds oneself. There is a kind of freedom here from the burdens of individuality together with an acuter sense of one's individuality as the person experiencing this extraordinary moment.

Indeed, this central thought about rapture is strongly suggested by the etymology of the word, coming as it does from the Latin *raptus*, a carrying off or abduction, and one might compare the modern meaning of "rapt," which suggests a deep, almost trance-like loss of self in some object. To be enraptured is to be taken out of oneself, lost in an experience, a sight, or whatever, and yet to be returned to oneself unburdened, with a sense of freedom.

This, then, is the model for rapture with which I work in this book: a loss of the self, a being taken out of oneself, and at the same time an intense return to the self—an awakening to the self that is also the self's freedom or liberation. I think, in fact, that we can see just this in Woolf's example: in her writing, she gets things right, and there is a kind of impersonality in this—things ought to be thus and so, and they are such; but there is the sense too that *she* has effected this, a kind of joy or delight in her own capacities and power.

I do not, of course, mean in speaking of this as a model of rapture to provide a *definition* of this notion. I mean it rather as a central case or example of rapture, a point of departure for thinking about it and its place in our life. And my aim in what follows is to explore a number of examples of rapture, experiences where this loss of self and return to self are present, and where some kind of pleasure or joy or delight is bound up with the experience.

But, as I explore each example, things usually become more complicated, and at times I link rapture to, for example, the experience of pain, or to experience that threatens pain, or to some other notion that one might have supposed tangential to it. Hence, for example, in discussing Werner Herzog's film about the ski jumper Steiner, I discuss the fact that the Steiner's rapture as he flies is connected with his sense that he is exposing himself to extreme danger, indeed to death. And so this theme then finds its place in my discussion. Or again, in my discussion I explore briefly the role pity plays in (some of) Herzog's films. The aim here is not to claim that in order to understand the notion of rapture one must always bring in the concept of pity. The idea is only that reflection on rapture as Herzog explores it invites one into thinking about pity in his films, and that that is significant, I take it, since many filmmakers may explore the notion of rapture without pity's ever being thematized at all in their work. What I am doing then, in such discussion, is trying to display how various concepts hang together in a *specific* context, without being anxious about showing the way in which they relate to one another *here* to be something one might suppose oneself to be able to find elsewhere—one might, or one might not. I take it that this is a version of what Wittgenstein called in a different context providing an *übersichtliche Darstellung*, usually translated as a "perspicuous representation," of a given concept.

But there is another aspect to my discussion. For hitherto I have spoken of specific experiences of rapture. Yet I think that there are certain lives that are, so to speak, lived under the sign of rapture or in the spirit of rapture. I think of these as emblematic lives, visions of the possibility of life by which we might be nourished and, perhaps, enabled to make space for, be better able to welcome into our own life, moments of being, moments of rapture. Such lives, for sure, no doubt have their fair share of the "cotton wool" that characterizes the life of the rest of us. This is why I speak of them as lived in the *spirit* of rapture: the idea here is not that of the experiences of a life that could be characterized as permanently marked by rapture, as if the person in question lived always in such a state, but of a life as, so to speak, *colored* by, lived in *the light of*, the notion of rapture.

Now, although philosophers are in general inattentive to the spirit in which individuals live, as they are, incidentally, to connected matters, such as an individual's temperament and style, this remains crucial for our understanding of each other. Indeed, these matters seem to me to be the ground on which we most immediately experience the people around us and the context for understanding their character traits, despite the fact that philosophers usually talk as if the character traits of an individual are the things most fundamental in our understanding and appreciation of that person. This seems to me to be a very flattened perspective on human life and false to our experience of each other. There may be many reasons why philosophers tend to take such a view, but primary here, I think, is the fact that, as Nietzsche pointed out, philosophers are often overly anxious to understand things in moralizing terms. Character traits look like the kind of thing that might be susceptible to moral education, and this is how philosophers often talk of them. The spirit in which someone lives looks much less likely as a candidate for moral education. Indeed, what is obvious is that, to take our notion of rapture, a person who lives in a spirit of rapture and who is admirable in this

5

sense might be far from being a *morally* admirable person: his or her excellence might reside largely elsewhere. This can be seen in, for example, the case of D. H. Lawrence, who lived in such a manner. He staked his all on a certain kind of moral integrity, but it was precisely a kind of integrity that cut in many ways against the sort of vision of morality to which so much moral philosophy seems committed—a vision central to which are the virtues that enable us to get on frictionlessly in our bourgeois "administered society," as Theodor Adorno put it.

Lawrence lived with a kind of energy for *life*, a willingness and ability to take life by the scruff of the neck and live it to the full. This is central to my sense that he lived in a spirit of rapture. Again, I intend this example as a kind of model for rapture from this point of view. Others who lived in this spirit may bear to Lawrence, and to each other, "family resemblances" in this respect, to invoke again a notion from Wittgenstein's thinking from another context. The artist Francis Bacon comes to mind here, at any rate as we find him in Michael Peppiatt's biography of him, *Francis Bacon in Your Blood*. Something similar might be said of Gabriele D'Annunzio, judging by Lucy Hughes-Hallett's biography of him, *The Pike: Gabriele D'Annunzio, Poet, Seducer and Preacher of War*.

As I have said, none of these individuals strikes me as being, at any rate in some conventional sense, particularly morally admirable. Indeed, D'Annunzio was positively dangerous. Nor do I wish to claim that their living in a spirit of rapture is necessarily the best way for a human being to live, however admirable I might find them. There are many other ways of living that are quite different and

6

that seem to me at least as admirable, perhaps more so. Primo Levi, for example, who lived a life that one might think of as a paradigm of depth, did not live in a spirit of rapture. Neither did Samuel Johnson, who is in my view one of the most admirable human beings who have ever lived.

For the most part, I explore in this book *moments* of rapture, but the idea of a life lived in the spirit of rapture informs my discussion at many points, particularly in the chapter in which I discuss Nietzsche's ill health and move from there to some comments on his philosophy overall. And I explore one specific life led in the spirit of rapture, that of Philippe Petit, the high-wire walker, in the final chapter.

▶ ▷ ▶

Hannah Arendt drew a distinction between discussion and conversation. A discussion, she says, aims at a conclusion; it aims to settle to things, to find an answer. A discussion aims to bring itself to an end for, once the conclusion is reached, once things are settled, there is nothing else to say. A conversation, however, is not like this. It does not aim at a conclusion, and it does not want to bring itself to an end. The pleasure of the conversation is in large part the pleasure of speaking with this specific person; it is also the pleasure of simply sharing thoughts, ideas, hopes, and wishes with him or her. The conversation ends simply when it is abandoned or runs out of steam. It serves no purposes other than itself, and its aims are all internal to it. It stimulates and interests, but it does not wish to prove or insist. It is open-ended and open-textured.

In reality, of course, a discussion may contain passages of conversation in the sense I have just adumbrated; and a conversation may harbor moments of discussion in the relevant sense. Nonetheless, the basic distinction is helpful because it draws attention to two quite different ways in which one can conceive of what one is doing in talking with another and, with that, different senses of who or what one takes one's interlocutor to be.

The basic distinction between discussion and conversation can be modeled, of course, in writing. And there is no doubt that most philosophy is written in the spirit of a discussion, not a conversation. It aims to convince the reader of a specific point of view or claim and to leave the reader with the sense that truth has been secured, the problem resolved. Such a view of philosophy expresses the philosopher's sense that he or she has the truth and will impart it in the argument offered to the reader, who will accordingly be convinced. The reader, on this understanding, figures for the philosopher as simply an intelligence to convince. Indeed, the philosopher takes himself or herself as an intellect that seeks to convince. On this understanding, neither the philosopher nor the reader is a whole human being with all that this entails by way of hope, fear, longing, fantasy, blood, sweat, and tears, with a largely obscure and confusing inner life, recalcitrant to improvement and stubborn in its obsessions and desires.

I aim in this book to write in the spirit of conversation, not discussion. I should like the book to be a record of an attempt to think through an understanding of rapture, all the while aware that someone else might approach matters quite differently and with insights I have missed, and, of course, exploring thinkers, writers, and filmmakers other than those whom I have chosen. For I am keenly aware that there are numerous people whose work might repay study in this context, and if I have not explored them, it is simply because I have sought to concentrate on those about whom I hope to have something helpful to say. To that extent, my choices are bound to be somewhat arbitrary, and I certainly have no wish at all to claim any special authority for them. Had I had the space to do so and the confidence that I might have had something worth saying about them, I should certainly have wanted to explore the work of Akira Kurosawa, Yukio Mishima, Clarice Lispector, Louise Glück, Jessica Hausner, and many others—others, perhaps, from cultural backgrounds very different from mine and from those of the individuals I do discuss here. Perhaps I shall do so on another occasion, and perhaps my reflections may have taken a different turn had I been able to expand the range here. For the moment, I can only hope that I have something interesting to say about those whom I have chosen, something that might provide the reader with some ideas for productive thought. But I claim no special insight into some final truth—even supposing, what is doubtful, that one can speak of truth in this way in this context. I have sought in this book merely to be as sensitive as I can to the issues I explore, and any authority I have in such matters comes not from anything I can *demand* of the reader, but rather from his or her sense that what I have to say rings true, strikes a chord, is helpful, or makes confusion more productive. I do not, in fact, think that philosophy ever does more than this, despite philosophers' claim (usually implicit; sometimes explicit) to the contrary.

My model for how to do philosophy in this register is Montaigne. Montaigne never tries to speak for the reader;

he is content to try to work out a thought for himself, obviously enough under the impact of his immense reading, learning, and life experience, but, when he has got things a little clearer for himself, he leaves things there. He claims no final truth for his views and thus believes what he believes in a spirit of skepticism, offering his ideas to the reader not to convince but to open things up and make one look again at what one thought was so clear but, under the impact of Montaigne's reflections, turns out not to be so at all. He speaks to the reader as to a friend, not an adversary, and he knows that, to get a person's intellectual assent to some idea is as nothing compared to allowing the idea to work into the other's whole being and become part, even if only a small part, of his total way of experiencing himself and the world.

Of course, no one can imitate Montaigne's writing style, and it would be foolish even to try to do so. But what one can do is learn from how unanxious he is. If he seeks to persuade us of something, he does this not by telling us what to think but by exploring what is *at stake* in a given thought—what it might mean in a human life, what it might illuminate, how it might become important, or too important, to us, become an object of obsession or fear, and so on. He gives his reasons for thinking what he thinks and then leaves us to explore that idea in the fabric of our lives. For sure, that relies on the thought that we are basically well-intentioned, not hard of heart, resolutely stubborn, and so on. We have to be open to the idea that we might not know, open to a different point of view, to being challenged. But that is a completely reasonable demand. Montaigne would not expect his ideas to cut any ice with those who are deeply dogmatic or corrupt or simply thoughtless.

He would have thought it just foolish to expect the significance, meaning, truth of a thought to be available to any
and everyone, even the most benightedly prejudiced, a fantasy of the power of thought and not a realistic expectation
about its place in human life.

So my aim in this book is to write in such a spirit, as
unanxiously as possible. In that sense, the chapters of this
book are written with a genuinely essayistic approach:
meditative, exploratory, as undogmatic as possible. I hope
simply to open up some lines of inquiry, inviting the reader
into a conversation. This is the kind of philosophy most to
my taste, and it is, I think, the kind of philosophy most
responsive to Socrates's claim at the foundation of Western thought that the one thing he knew was that he knew
nothing.

I spoke earlier about the possibility, through reflecting on
the experience of rapture, of being able to find more space
for moments of rapture in one's life, and I certainly hope
to draw attention in this book to this. But sometimes my
aim has been—perhaps at the same time—simply to draw
attention to the ways in which others have found or made
such space in their lives. There may be no implication here
that one can then do much or anything in the light of such
a possibility in others to make or find such space in one's
own life. Or there may be. That is the point. For all will
depend here on what the example is and who is reflecting
on it. I may be able to find room for something more in
my life by reflecting on some specific example, while you
may not—or vice versa, of course. But beyond the idea of

11

finding space in one's life for something more, or something else, I want in this book also simply to draw attention to the richness of life in exploring the examples I offer. One can simply feel a sense of *coming alive* through being in contact with these examples, as one can come alive, for example, in reading great imaginative literature or watching an absorbing and surprising film or contemplating a marvelous painting or the like. Here it is a matter of being vivified by this contact—and it may be nothing more. But that, to my mind, is already a lot—perhaps because that *is*, after all, in a sense, a way of making space in one's life for a moment of rapture. Nietzsche said that Montaigne made life worth living, and I think he meant by that that reading Montaigne made him feel he had come alive, whether or not he was able directly to absorb into his life anything of the way Montaigne lived—say, living with more equanimity of spirit. But then, Nietzsche did, after all, absorb Montaigne into his life, however indirectly. And if someone asked me how this was so, given that he notably failed to change his life at all in the light of Montaigne's thought and life, I would say that the answer is simply that he *loved* him. That *is* the change—a change that is no change at all, one might say. That is in itself a great gift.

Be that as it may, there is more to be said. Someone might, for example, contemplating Petit's life, feel a kind of resentment or disappointment, since he or she may sense that this immensely exuberant and even reckless way of living is in one way admirable but feel that all it does is to cast light on his or her own limitedness, or limitations, even leaving aside the issue of whether there is any carryover from Petit's life to his or her own. Witnessing

12

another's life so full of rapturous energy may make one feel all the more one's own impoverishment. In fact, I actually felt this way when I read Peppiatt's biography of Francis Bacon, mentioned earlier. In light of Bacon's life, I had a sense of my own as unbelievably tame and mediocre. I had no temptation to dismiss his life for this reason or feel resentment, but I could understand someone who did: seeing another's intensely energetic engagement with life can make one feel that he or she is running past and kicking sand in one's eyes. There is no guarantee at all that some of the examples I explore will not evoke such a reaction in some of those who think about them. I hope this is not so, but I can see no way around taking the risk other than avoiding the issue at all. And, relatedly, I have no general answer to the question, which I mentioned earlier and to which I shall return, of how it is that the experience of rapture, which can be indifferent to morality, can mesh with the demands others legitimately place on us or with our obligations to them. But I do not think that there *is* a general answer. If one does find an answer, that answer will be one's life—which does not mean, of course, that others may not think one's answer very bad.

▶ ▷ ▶

If it makes sense to think of making space in one's life for the experience or moments of rapture, this inevitably raises the question of one's self-consciousness in the making of that space. It is a well-known and deeply troubling aspect of our condition that the pursuit of happiness is likely to inhibit our actually achieving it. "Nothing is more

hopeless than a scheme of merriment," remarked Samuel Johnson and, even if he is not right about every such
scheme, the point is well-taken. If you set things up in an
attempt to be happy, you are likely to be disappointed,
partly because the very desire to be happy, straining after
it, so to speak, itself becomes a distraction from whatever it
was that you are doing that you thought would make you
happy. And in part the issue is one of the human imagination, which is always able to conceive of a felicity that
exceeds what reality offers. What one can do, however, is—
to put it roughly—forget about happiness and get interested in other things, for we find ourselves happiest, I
think, when the mind is absorbed in activities to which
it finds no resistance, which is why we speak of losing
ourselves in something—a game, a piece of reading, a
film, or whatever. For sure, one can certainly find oneself absorbed in something that one cannot reflectively
endorse—these days, for example, we all know how easy it
is to be absorbed by technology (the internet, smartphones,
and so on) yet feel that this is largely a waste of time—but
the general point still holds, I think, other things being
equal. And one oddity of losing oneself in something in
the way in question is that there is a sense in which one
does not notice it, precisely because one is absorbed. One
does not notice it, that is, as something that has an edge:
one is just there, with the object of interest, and time for
this reason does not weigh on one as it does when one is
unhappy—bored, frustrated, and the like. It is as if human
beings can be happy but can only see this on the edge of
their consciousness; move it to the center, and it evapo-
rates. Self-consciousness, one might say, is the enemy of

happiness. What is really at stake is being *open* to it *without pursuing* it.

I should say the same about rapture. As with happiness, pursuing rapture is likely to disable one's being able to find or experience it. So when I speak here about making space in one's life for moments of rapture, I mean that not in the sense of pursuing such moments, but rather simply being open to their possibility. A good example of this comes in my discussion in chapter 5 of Staff-Captain Ryabovich in Chekhov's short story "The Kiss." Ryabovich, lonely and unloved, cherishes all summer long a kiss that he has received from an unknown woman who mistook him for her lover. He is able to find such rapture in it in large part because it was so unexpected, not at all planned, not at all part of a "scheme of merriment." His openness to the possibility was not even something of which he was aware. But then he becomes aware—or, rather, self-aware. The whole summer long he yearns for the kiss again, and implicit in Chekhov's story is the sense that, even were he to find the woman in question and receive another kiss, it would be a disappointment because he has lived countless days with the imagined idea of what it would be to receive it. As it is, he never finds the woman in question, despite his longing and search, but Chekhov intimates a deeper sense that he can never have what he longs for so ardently.

This book, then, is not meant to be an invitation to the pursuit of rapture, whatever that would be exactly. It is meant to work, rather, as a reminder of a human possibility—a reminder as much to me as to anyone else. As so often in life, we need regularly to be reminded of what we know already but lose so easily from view. And in being

15

reminded, we may find things open up for us in unexpected ways.

▶ ▷ ▶

Philosophy has not, in general, had a great deal to say about rapture. Why is this?

I suspect that one reason is that the topic of rapture may appear to many philosophers—particularly, perhaps, contemporary philosophers who are, in general, steeped in naturalistic, nonreligious thought—as rather too close to being a matter of religion, perhaps specifically Christianity. For, of course, religion, not just Christianity, has great interest in, a commitment to, states of rapture: Sufism, Yom Kippur, Sukkot, asceticism, mystical transport, the dark night of the soul. All this and more in religion is a matter of rapture or closely related experiences. And then there is *the rapture*, an eschatological position held by some (evangelical) Christians. But none of that gets much attention in philosophy, which so often longs for order and shuns the extremes of life. These religious themes, and more, would certainly repay study in thinking about rapture, but I have not in this book concentrated on such religious forms of rapture, for I have wished to write from a broadly humanist point of view, that is, to try to show ways in which we might find or welcome moments of rapture into our lives even outside a religious context. The exception to this is chapter 6, in which I have sought to explore the theme of rapture in part by reflecting on some aspects of the thinking of Simone Weil, who pursued a very specific kind of Christian life. I should stress here that I am well aware that Weil's approach to Christianity—which revolved around a desire to free herself from the ego and become nothing, which she called "decreation"—is, indeed, but one way of understanding that specific religious outlook. There are many varieties of Christianity, and Weil's is one that stresses a strong distinction between flesh and spirit, her attempts at mediating the two in her reflections on the beauty of the material world not being, in the end, in my view, especially convincing. Other versions of Christianity are much less invested in this distinction than was Weil, and much friendlier to the material world than she was, and I hope that my chapter on her will be read in the light of that recognition even as, I am sure, my sense that there is something powerfully right about her reading of Christianity will no doubt come through in what I say.

But there is, I think, a second reason why philosophy has not shown itself much interested in the notion of rapture. For, from more or less its beginnings, Western philosophy has, as I have already intimated, been heavily invested in the idea of moral improvement, and it has often been supposed that either by being a philosopher or by being educated by a philosopher, one has some particular or special route toward that improvement. Socrates, on Plato's understanding, lived morally well because he was a philosopher, and, further, he was able to teach us how to do so. This is in part what Nietzsche meant when he said that philosophy comes to a halt before morality: it does not simply wish to understand human life but wishes to do so with moral intent. So, for example, it has long been an aspiration among many philosophers—the most notable exception among the great philosophers being Kant—to show that only if you are morally good can you really be happy. As Nietzsche tartly remarked, the wicked who are happy are a species about whom the moralists are silent.

Now, I share the hope that philosophy has something to teach about living well—living less wastefully or carelessly, with greater depth, insight, or wisdom. But I am not sure that living in that way always maps seamlessly onto our moral concerns. For sure, morality is important to us, but it is far from clear to me that living with greater depth and the rest really is (always?) a matter of morality: Could there not be ways of living that we can admire as exemplary in some way, without assuming that those ways must be morally good? Morality is no doubt important in different ways to all of us, but assuming it to be *the* central aspect of the good life is surely a very large assumption—or hope. Moreover, the moral intent of a great deal of philosophy seems to me often to lead to distortions and omissions: philosophy tends to back off in the face of lives that seem admirable but hardly morally special. In general, philosophers have not themselves often wished to display what is admirable in such individuals for fear, I suppose, of encouraging others to live in a similar way. Hence it is that Bernard Williams remarked that a great deal of philosophy has the "tireless aim of . . . [seeking] to make the world safe for well-disposed people."[4] And when Bertrand Russell commented, "Philosophers, for the most part, are constitutionally timid, and dislike the unexpected. Few of them would be genuinely happy as pirates or burglars," he was pointing out, among other things, the way in which philosophers tend to construct systems that reflect their own peculiar type of temperament, one, indeed, that would not, perhaps, lead them to be happy as a pirates or burglars.[5] Wanting a world that fits their timidity, Russell is saying, and finding

18

that the world is not like that at all, they construct one in their philosophy that matches their needs.

There is a great deal more one could say in exploration of all this, but perhaps we can now see why it is that rapture has not interested philosophers as much as one might have hoped or expected. For while the experience of rapture can be one that need not be hostile to moral concerns and demands, and indeed may express them, as is perhaps the case with Jean-Jacques Rousseau's stay on the island of La Motte, discussed in chapter 4, rapture is nonetheless likely to be disruptive in many of its forms to sound moral sense—and thus to be something suspicious to much philosophy. This is obvious from the model of rapture, as I am understanding it here, where sex provides the central example. For it is completely clear that sex is a force in human life that is often deeply recalcitrant to moral demands, challenging or overturning our moral commitments and desire for moral rectitude and order. More generally, rapture, as I mentioned earlier, expresses a kind of energy for life, something that can be exhilarating and can lead to a recklessness that is disrespectful of moral demands. Indeed, now we can see more clearly why it is that rapture can be connected with pain or with the risk of death. For, although we start with the idea that being in a state of rapture promises pleasure, it is clear that, precisely because it takes one out of oneself, because it can be deeply intoxicating, it can involve pain and suffering. From that point of view we might find that we speak of someone's being in a state of rapture when it is clear that he or she is undergoing something that is in part terrible. Othello's agony over Desdemona provides one good example. Heinrich von Kleist's appalling project to find a person with whom to commit suicide provides another such example, and he certainly was in a state of rapture when he wrote his farewell letters on the evening before he shot Henriette Vogel through the heart and then blew his own brains out. Or again, to advert once more to my discussion of Simone Weil in chapter 6, I explore her as someone who lived in a certain way in a state of rapturous self-destruction, and I relate this to a further example, that of Peter Bergmann, who, in an extremely elaborate planned gesture lasting a whole weekend, prepared for his own suicide in a way that would erase any evidence of his ever having lived.

It is striking that literature is, in general, much less anxious than philosophy is to look at things through a moral lens; less anxious, as it were, to tidy them up. The great novelists, poets, and playwrights no doubt have a vision of life, as Tony Tanner has remarked, but that is not the same as wanting to straighten things out:

> Every great writer has a vision; he creates a recognisable universe which contains selected raw material from the real world, intensified and transformed into art by the very power of that vision. He gives us reality saturated with insight, experience exposed by the passion of his own perspective. He does not bully us with a creed . . . rather he opens up unsettling areas of existence and shows us values in the making, and in the destroying.[6]

"Values in the making, and in the destroying": the great writer helps us to see what is at stake in commitment to, fascination by, longing for, fear of . . . certain values—values that may not be, in all probability will not be, at any rate not exclusively, *moral* values. And in doing this, he or

INTRODUCTION

she allows us space that it is rare to find in mainstream philosophy.

We can put the point this way. As I remarked, rapture can be a disruptive force because it is expressive of a certain energy for *life*. The experience of rapture is that of a hunger for experience, a hunger that can be, even if it need not always be, imperious and demanding. And in providing space for the exploration of such things, great writers give greater space than philosophy does for individuals to be themselves. For, even if I am invested in philosophy's aim to live with greater wisdom, even if I share philosophy's desire in this way, I am also aware that what it is to be me is to be a person with specific forms of unruliness, foolishness, imprudence, obsession, anger, and so on. If I were to lose these, I would lose myself, or part of myself that makes up what it is to be me, living this particular life. Even though these features of my being may be painful for me or others around me at least some of the time—may, let us say, be morally questionable—I may feel also that to lose them would be to find myself truncated, would be to lose a sense of my energy for life, my hunger for experience. Great literature does not aim to excise these from my being, even though some philosophers—importing into their understanding of literature their understanding of philosophy and seeing it through that lens—claim otherwise. Rather, it allows me to explore these and, perhaps, understand them better. It does not wish to moralize them out of existence. Indeed, literature can allow me to see these aspects of my being as something to be cherished and valued, forms of exuberant life—forms, indeed, perhaps, of rapture.

Each of us lives, I am saying, as many have said before, of course, with a deep tension: the tension between moral

21

demands, about which we care, and other things, other values, things that may matter to us as much as, perhaps at times more than, moral values. The art of living is in large part, I think, a negotiation between these, and no one can tell another the secret of how to do this in his or her case—for there is no such secret, just a constant working through. Puritanism is a claim to have the answer on one side; a kind of rampant letting go might be the claim on the other side. Neither is especially appealing, and neither is a viable option for most of us. But I think that philosophy sometimes supposes that there is a secret and it can reveal it. At more or less the outset of philosophy, Aristotle tells us as much when he says that he is able to reveal to us a life that is "complete and lacking in nothing"—lacking, he means, of course, in nothing that really matters. Before Aristotle, Plato had his own answer to what that might be. I think that literature helps remind us that these claims to knowledge, and others by many other philosophers, are an illusion, and it does this by reminding us of what philosophy leaves out too frequently—which we could call, indeed, the rapture of life. This is certainly not to say that one cannot learn much from philosophy. But so far as those philosophers are concerned who have elaborated explanatory systems of existence, it is usually from the thoughts, ideas, and suggestions explored and elaborated along the way, and in the asides and minor comments or remarks, that we can learn the most, not from the system as a whole, which in the end, I think, always looks contrived or forced. And this returns me to the idea of philosophy in a conversational mode. For if I am right about where one can learn the most from the great philosophical systems—in, so to speak, the interstices—then one is likely to think that a better way to write philosophy is precisely by prescinding from any kind of system and writing philosophy that has the unsystematic nature of life itself—as literature, at any rate in many of its forms, does. Kierkegaard wrote a book with the title *Philosophical Fragments*, and whatever he meant exactly by invoking the idea of fragments, the notion appeals to my sense of what philosophy can be: fragments that one can pick up and put down, compare with each other, rearrange so that one can see them better. And this is what I have hoped to provide here: some fragments illuminating the concept of rapture for further conversation.

1
Nietzsche

Illness and Italy

Philosophers have written countless books and articles
on Friedrich Nietzsche. Most of those books and articles ignore the man for the work, even though he thought
that this was a wholly inadequate way to read philosophers'
writings, did not read them himself in that way, and made
it clear that others should not read him as if he were one
thing and his books another. He would certainly be repelled
by what the academic industry has made of him, turning
him into another philosopher of the tradition, when all he
wanted to do was to destroy that tradition and stop philosophers going about things as they always had done. But he
would not be surprised at that, I think, despite the fact
that, for all his insistence on adopting a resolutely tough,
unillusioned view of life, he was often rather naïve. In any
case, with or without the naïveté, the whole thing would
have only embedded further in him the disgust with human
beings that assailed him throughout his life, and to which
he was morbidly, miserably attached.

What manner of man was he? He was an *écorché vif:* he suffered in body and mind from the world everywhere he went, was overwhelmed by it, horrified by its endless spectacle of stupidity and brutality. He was oversensitive, troubled, wounded, and consumed by a longing for freedom from all this: vast swathes of his writing are attempts to free himself from his oversensitivity, forms of fantasy or hope, dreams, and longings, which most philosophers have misread as if they were objective arguments, detachable from the man's life, rather than cries of agony and desire.

It is impossible to know where his spiritual and psychological sufferings began and the physical ailments from which he suffered all his life—eclipsing migraines, stomach cramps, poor eyesight verging at times on blindness—ended. Well, there is no beginning and no end: Nietzsche's sufferings make a mockery of the idea that we can keep the categories of the spiritual and the physical apart.

Nietzsche owed everything to his illness, even as he longed to be free of it.

In 1886 he wrote second prefaces to a number of his works, including to his book *Die fröhliche Wissenchaft*, originally published in 1882. The preface to this book, whose title is usually rendered in English these days as *The Gay Science*, not least because Nietzsche added the alternative Italian title *La gaya scienza* to the work, is of extreme interest. It is so because its leading theme is that of the rapture Nietzsche experienced as he recovered, however briefly, from a particularly intense period of illness. Gratitude, he tells us, pours forth from the book, the gratitude of one who, contrary to all expectations, is now recovered. Suddenly the future seems open to him, suddenly he is able to play, to be foolish, to joke. Nietzsche is *drunk* with the sense of his recovery.

This sense of immense release from the anxious, suffering self, this opening out and self-loss—which is also a self-recovery, of course—reminds us, as it reminded Nietzsche, of the immense profundity of the experience of illness.

> Out of such abysses, out of such profound illness, also out of the illness of deep suspicion, one comes back *newborn*, having shed one's skin, more ticklish and malicious, with a finer taste for joy, with a tenderer tongue for all good things, with merrier senses, with a second more dangerous innocence in joy, more childlike, and a hundred times more sophisticated than one was before.[1]

Shedding one's skin: the image is one of achieved freshness, of growth, and of something expansive and free. It connects, of course, with the crucial ideas of being newborn, more childlike. For children, the world is *new*; everything is novel. We know that, as adults, it is rarely possible to keep this sense of novelty alive, to have a sense of the world as fresh and new. This is not, or need not be, at any rate, a matter of being jaded or cynical; it is a matter of being *habituated* to things. We know what it is to crave the new, and perhaps the problem is especially acute for those of us who live in the bloated but decaying late-capitalist world—a world of surfeit, where we gorge ourselves so readily on all that it offers by way of pleasure and entertainment and yet are left so often with a sense of emptiness or frustration. Emerging from illness—especially, perhaps,

27

when the emergence is unexpected—allows us for a moment to be free of our supersaturated self and reclaim a feeling for the newness of the world. Our eyes are as if opened for the first time, our senses expansive and receptive, and we suddenly are able to appreciate the small and seemingly insignificant things that, after all, we discover, are among the most significant.

Nietzsche expresses this in a desire, or hope, that he will be able to live on the surface of life: to stop at the skin, he says. The skin, the surface: Nietzsche invites us into thinking of his rapture in these terms.

Clearly the notion of the skin captured Nietzsche's imagination. The skin is the point of interface between the world and one's being, and Nietzsche conceptualizes the skin as the point at which his body and the world become one: we normally think of the skin as the point at which I end and the world begins; Nietzsche conceives of it as the place at which he and the world flow back and forth into each other, porous to each other, wholly responsive the one to the other. In his state of recovery, his body is at one with the body of the world.

In a piece of writing that is supposed to be a piece of neutral, sober metaphysics, but which, in fact, gets out of hand and becomes a lyrical paean to existence, to the human being in existence, in the world, Maurice Merleau-Ponty says this: "One can say that we perceive the things themselves, that we are the world that thinks itself—or that the world is at the heart of our flesh." "The world," he says, "is universal flesh." "The flesh," he goes on,

> is not matter, is not mind, is not substance. To designate it, we should need the old term "element," in the sense it was

used to speak of water, air, earth, and fire, that is, in the sense of a *general thing*, mid-way between the spatio-temporal individual and the idea, a sort of incarnate principle that brings a style of being wherever there is a fragment of being. The flesh is in this sense an "element" of being.[2]

Even if Merleau-Ponty's analysis is correct, it can hardly be denied, I think, that we do not experience our body in this way, as at one with the flesh of the world, as the flesh of the world, most of the time. Rather, we are *over here* and the world is *over there*, set against us, even if momentarily amenable to our purposes and aims. But the experience of being newborn, in Nietzsche's sense, is, I think, an experience in which we *feel* the world as Merleau-Ponty says it is all the time. Nietzsche has the experience, the *feeling*, of stopping at the surface of the world, at the surface of his body, at the skin of world and body; he is his flesh, he is the world's flesh, the world's flesh is his—is what he is. It is a rapturous moment.

One lesson that Nietzsche draws from this is, as I noted earlier, the importance of attentiveness to the small things in life. I imagine his thought as this: in recovering from illness, I suddenly become attentive to the small things in life, to their irreplaceable value, and then I grasp that these are things that are a source of value in life generally. So, emerging from a period of illness is one of the central experiences that opens us up to an appreciation of the value of small things in life, and these then come to occupy a much greater place in one's "table of values," to use a phrase to which Nietzsche was much attached, more generally. This explains why he returns again and again to the importance of the small and minor details of life in living well.

Earthly frailties and their main cause.—When one looks about one, one is forever coming across people who have eaten eggs all their lives without noticing that the oblong-shaped ones have the best taste; who do not know that a thunderstorm is good for the abdomen; that pleasant smells are strongest in cold, clear air; that our sense of taste varies in different parts of the mouth; that every meal at which we talk well or listen well does harm to the digestion. Even if these examples of a lack of power of observation appear inadequate, one will nevertheless readily grant that most people see very imperfectly, very rarely pay attention to, those things that are *closest* to them. Is that unimportant [*gleichgültig*]?—One should reflect, however, that *almost all physical and mental frailties* of the individual stem from this lack. Not to know what is beneficial and what harmful to us in the organisation of our life [*in der Einrichtung der Lebensweise*], division of the day, time and choice of company, in work [*Beruf*] and leisure, commanding and obeying, feeling for nature and art, eating, sleeping and reflecting; to be *unknowledgeable concerning the smallest and most everyday things* and not to be sharp sighted—it is this that makes the earth for so many a "vale of tears."[3]

And: "These small things—nutrition, place, climate, rest, the whole casuistry of selfishness—are far more important than everything one has taken to be important so far."[4] Also: "Precisely the least thing, the quietest, lightest, the rustling of a lizard, a breath, a whoosh, a glance of the eye—it takes little to make up the quality of the *best* happiness. Soft!"[5]

Here, perhaps, we see most clearly Nietzsche's sense of being at one with the world, or longing for this to be so, expressed as a reflection on his philosophy:

Circuitous Routes.—At what does this whole philosophy aim with all its circuitous routes? Does it do more than transpose into reason, so to speak, a steady and strong drive [*Trieb*]—a longing [*Trieb*] for mild sun, a bright and bracing air, southern plants, the smell of the sea, short meals of meat, eggs, and fruit, hot water to drink, quiet day-long hikes, little talking, occasional and cautious reading, living alone, pure, simple, and almost soldierly habits—in short, for all things which are suited to my own personal taste, that are most beneficial to me? A philosophy which is fundamentally the instinct for a personal diet? An instinct that seeks for my air, my heights, my climate [*Witterung*], and my kind of health, and passes along the circuitous route of my mind [*Umweg meines Kopfes*]?[6]

There is something provocative in Nietzsche's thinking on this matter of the small things of life. In telling us that these things are more important than those matters that have usually been taken to be so, he is saying something that will astonish, and probably irritate, anyone who is used to philosophy's usual understanding of what really counts, for philosophy typically disdains discussion of such matters, preferring to concentrate on other things: God, morality, political justice, tragedy, and so on. And of course, life being what it is, Nietzsche certainly spent a great deal of time attending to the traditional concerns of philosophy, despite his occasional pretense to be indifferent to them. Still, for all that, there is immense value in what he says, for it is surely true that one of the things that can make life so much less than it could be is our quotidian mismanagement of our life, our inattentiveness to the small things of life. For there is, I think, a kind of quiet rapture in getting things right here.

▶ ▷ ▶

In a brilliant essay on illness, Virginia Woolf suggests some thoughts that complement Nietzsche's reflections as we have been tracing them so far.

Woolf points out that illness can draw us in two opposing directions at once. On the one hand, one is drawn to one's body, which becomes the center of one's attention; one is isolated from others, in one's body. On the other hand, one's attention can be drawn to the world in unexpected ways. Her example is attention to the sky.

> The first impression of that extraordinary spectacle [of the sky] is strangely overcoming. Ordinarily to look at the sky for any length of time is impossible. Pedestrians would be impeded and disconcerted by a public sky-gazer. What snatches we get of it are mutilated by chimneys and churches, serve as a background for man, signify wet weather or fine, daub windows gold, and, filling in the branches, complete the pathos of dishevelled autumnal plane trees in autumnal squares. Now, lying recumbent, staring straight up, the sky is discovered to be something so different from this that really it is a little shocking. This then has been going on all the time without our knowing it!—this incessant making up of shapes and casting them down, this buffeting of clouds together, and drawing vast trains of ships and waggons from North to South, this incessant ringing up and down of curtains of light and shade, this interminable experiment with gold shafts and

blue shadows, with veiling the sun and unveiling it, with
making rock ramparts and wafting them away—this endless activity, with the waste of Heaven knows how many
million horse power of energy, has been left to work its will
year in year out.[7]

Of course, much will depend on the nature of the illness from which one is suffering as to whether the body or
the surrounding world occupies most of one's attention.
But Woolf's point is that in many illnesses there will be an
alternation, an equivocation, a subtle dialectical interplay
between the two foci. It is not just, as Nietzsche says, that
the world becomes new to us as we recover from illness; it
can also become new to us even as we are ill. Illness is
itself, or can be if one is lucky, something that gives one a
kind of oneness with the world.

Yet the world stops when one is ill. I lie for days pros-
trate and then, finally, leave the home or hospital and am
amazed that all this is going on. "Mrs Jones catches her
train. Mr Smith mends his motor. The cows are driven
home to be milked. Men thatch the roof. The dogs bark.
The rooks, rising in a net, fill in a net upon the elm trees.
The wave of life flings itself out indefatigably."[8] All this is
going on, has been going on, while I lay recumbent, consumed by my body, staring at the spectacle of the sky! I
thought the world had come to a standstill with me!

But perhaps Nietzsche's illness was too great to allow
him to see the sky as if for the first time. Nonetheless, he
certainly saw it when he recovered.

Nietzsche wrote his second preface in Italy. He was in
Ruta, near Genoa. Later, he spent some time in Turin, a
city that filled him with joy, a kind of abandon in pleasure.

I know Nietzsche's feeling, including his feeling for, and in, Italy. In 2011 I was suffering in the first months of the year from various illnesses: migraines, dizziness, pins and needles, shortness of breath. . . . The doctors could find nothing. At the beginning of July in that year I went to Bologna in Italy for six months. I was immediately well again. I experienced the same openness to the world as did Nietzsche in Ruta and in Turin. The warmth and sun; the endless blue sky; the light on the red stones of the buildings; the porticoes offering protection from the heat; the endless hidden corners, unexpected *piazze*, cafés, and bars; the youth and vitality of the inhabitants; the sense of a city at once modern and yet lost somewhere in the early twentieth century before its horrors; the compact, elegant roads leading away from the city to magnificent parks and gardens, orchards and streams; all this and more made being in Bologna like permanently lounging under a tree on the lawn on a warm summer's afternoon. The ease I experienced in Bologna is unparalleled in my life, an ease all the more astounding in that, far from making me lethargic, it gave me renewed energy for my work. I felt there as I had never felt before, and I have not felt since, as if I had come into a patrimony of immense wealth, a kind of surfeit of delight. Keats celebrated life in much of his poetry as a sensuous glut. In Bologna, I knew what he meant.

And I knew what Merleau-Ponty meant too. I felt in Bologna as if the city were knowing itself, thinking itself, feeling itself through me—not in a spirit of self-absorption, but in one of gratitude. I discovered my physical being in Bologna, my being made of flesh, in Merleau-Ponty's terms, even as I discovered the city. I think that my being ill before arriving was crucial to this discovery.

► ▷ ►

I have so far focused on Nietzsche's recovery from illness. But in reflecting on his ill health itself, he links it intimately with philosophy:

> One will note that I do not want to bid farewell to that time of severe illness with ingratitude, the benefit of which I have today still not fully exhausted: I am very conscious of the advantages my unreliable health gives me. . . . A philosopher who has over and again made his way through many kinds of health has also made his way through an equal number of philosophies: he *cannot but* transmute his condition every time into a spiritual form and distance— this transfiguration just *is* philosophy.[9]

Many philosophers would disagree with Nietzsche concerning the nature of philosophy as he expresses it here. Or perhaps most of them would not so much disagree as not know what to make of what he says, finding this claim about illness and philosophy so absurd or wild as hardly to know what to say in reply, what to do with the comment. Philosophy, they might say, is a matter of sober and objective analysis of the relations between concepts, of the nature and conditions governing our claims to knowledge or the fundamental ontology of the human condition, and illness has nothing much (interesting; deep) to do with all that.

But two things need to be said. First, we should see Nietzsche here as offering his illness to us as a gift. He wants to give us his illness, but not, of course, in its raw state. He wants to show us how he was grateful to it and how he made sense of it, found meaning in it. Second, he wants to do this because he thinks of human beings as creatures who are ill. We live, he thinks, between the demands of culture, demands for order and discipline, and those of our "animal" nature, antisocial, chaotic, sometimes violent drives. These drives are a constant reminder of, expression of, our nature as embodied creatures, animals with a body. Our fundamental illness is that conflict, and the other illnesses to which we are subject—such as the specific ones that afflicted Nietzsche—are, for Nietzsche, a form of recall to the body and to the deeply troubling nature we possess *as such* as creatures with a body. Nietzsche, in other words, sees a continuity between the specific illnesses to which any given person is subject and the fundamental illness that we possess, that we *are*, as the kind of creature we are. In either case, we are recalled to the body and required to seek meaning in the illness, grasping it as something central to what we are. Nietzsche is resisting the idea that health is the *opposite* of illness, if that means that when we are healthy we are no longer ill. Rather, he thinks, we are always ill—"man is the sick animal," as he puts it—and that health is a modulated form of illness, and vice versa, of course.

Put in those terms, it is far from obvious that Nietzsche is wrong to claim that philosophy is the transfiguration of illness.

No one has brought out better this intertwining of health and illness in Nietzsche than Stefan Zweig. Having

described Nietzsche's endless agonies—"headaches, numb-
ing blinding headaches . . . stomach cramps and vomiting
of blood, migraines, fever, loss of appetite, exhaustion,
haemorrhoids, constipation, shivering, night sweats"—he
then notes that Nietzsche writes, referring to the last fif-
teen years of his life, in his bizarre autobiography *Ecce
Homo*: "*Summa summarum* I have been well." Which is
true, asks Zweig, the endless agony or that monumental
assertion? Both!

> Nietzsche's body was constitutionally tough and resistant,
> like a widely-arching tree, capable of bearing the heaviest
> load; its roots went deep into the soil of the healthy Ger-
> man pastors from whom he was descended. As a whole
> "*summa summarum,*" deep down, as an organism, at the very
> basis of his spiritual and material being, Nietzsche really
> was healthy. But his nerves were too delicate for the vio-
> lence of his feelings and so were permanently in revolt.[10]

Nietzsche was profoundly ill and profoundly healthy at
the same time, and there is, for us, a kind of horrified fascination in witnessing his monumental struggle with himself and the world around him. We see him and marvel
that a life can be like this. As in the case of Samuel Johnson, who, like Nietzsche, suffered appallingly and said, late
in life, that he had never known a day free of pain, we wonder at the immense fortitude that allowed these men, not
simply to bear their agony, but to *turn it to account*.

Nietzsche, then, gives us the gift of his illness—
transfigured into philosophy—that we might learn to
make sense of, find meaning in, our own illness. He also,
as we saw earlier, gave us his desire for a certain personal

regimen transmuted into philosophy. Illness and health; health and illness.

When I first read Nietzsche many years ago, I experienced a kind of rapture that, I think, is common to many who come to him for the first time. There are certainly many reasons for that, including his mastery of language, his passion, his boldness, and so on. But I also think that a central reason for such a reaction is that one senses on first reading Nietzsche, however inchoately, that here we are in the presence of a philosopher who is fully *there*, a man of flesh and blood, a whole human being, thinking not just with his mind but with his whole body—in the marrow bone, as Yeats has it. And it is his illness that is key to that presence—his transfiguration of his illness into philosophy. By comparison with Nietzsche, the philosophers I had read before suddenly appeared desiccated, overly cautious, lacking in energy and vitality, pedantic, timid. The sense of relief was overwhelming: this was why I had wanted to study philosophy!

Of course, I realize now that some of this was youthful indiscipline on my part, but I remain convinced that one reason that so many continue to be fascinated by Nietzsche is the reason I had for finding him so exciting to read when I was very young. But what is odd is that, with a few exceptions, one finds little of that excitement in most of the philosophy written about him. Nietzsche's writings are full of wild exaggerations, expressions of different moods—joy, despair, disgust, longing, terror and much else, jokes (most of them fairly bad), mockery, flights of fancy . . . and it is far from clear how this connects with the more sober moments of his work, how integral they are to them, whether they can be detached without loss from the rest,

and so on. Yet most of that hardly gets into the philosophical interpretations of Nietzsche: most philosophers simply
do not know what to do with it. And this is one central
reason why, when one turns from Nietzsche to those who
write on him, one so often has a sense that the very thing
that made him so exciting in the first place has been left out.
One way to put this is to say that the rapture of reading
Nietzsche rarely if ever gets into the pages of those who
write about him; yet it was this that drew them to him in
the first place. Philosophy analyzes, dissects, makes dis-
tinctions, reduces, and, in doing so, finds it has no room
for the experience that can underpin it in the first place. E.
M. Cioran makes the point brilliantly:

39

> I turned away from philosophy when it became impossi-
> ble to discover in Kant any human weakness, any authen-
> tic accent of melancholy; in Kant and in all the philoso-
> phers.... We cannot elude existence by explanations, we
> can only endure it, love or hate it, adore or dread it, in that
> alternation of happiness and horror which expresses the
> very rhythm of being, its oscillations, its dissonances, its
> bright or bitter vehemences.... We do not *argue* the uni-
> verse; we *express* it. And philosophy does not express
> it. The real problems begin only after having ranged or
> exhausted it.... The philosopher... [is] the enemy of
> disaster... sane as reason itself, and as prudent.... We
> begin to live authentically only where philosophy ends, at
> its wreck.[11]

Nietzsche would without doubt have agreed with this, and
he did all he could to shake philosophy up from the inside.
He certainly failed in that, and, as I noted at the outset of

this chapter, he has largely been co-opted into a kind of discourse he wished to undermine. His problem was this: if you criticize philosophy from the inside, speaking in the terms current in the discipline, you cannot really shake things up because, in speaking in those terms, you effectively lose the critical point you want to make; but if you speak in terms that philosophers do not recognize, they will think you are not properly engaging with them and will feel that they can ignore you with impunity. Nietzsche was driven to paroxysms of anger by this, because he grasped that *whatever* he said and *however* he said it, he would, one way or another, be misunderstood. This anger too was his illness, and he gave it to us in his work.

There is, nonetheless, an immensely *tonic* effect in Nietzsche's anger. It is like getting a shot in the arm of a powerful drug that sends one reeling, intoxicated and thrilled, and not quite sure where one is. This is certainly something he wanted to achieve with his writings. There is a sense in reading him that he *expresses* the universe, as Cioran suggests our deepest engagement with it should.

So now something else comes into view. The whole of Nietzsche's philosophy is, in a way, an antiphilosophy. He does not want, as so many philosophers have, to recruit philosophy to the task of educating us morally. When he speaks of his recovery from illness and his sense of gratitude to and for life in this moment, he means this as one instance of what he thinks of as the Dionysiac, a rapturous energy for life as a whole. This is why his work is full of explorations of anger, disgust, horror, mischief, playfulness, joy, and so on: he wants us to be able to acknowledge these as part of our life, give them the space they demand, a space that we deny them only at risk of paying the price of becoming enervated. And this explains his relentless hostility to morality: he sees morality as the enemy of those forces and thus as something that risks making us give up on life, lose our sense of why it is worth being alive at all. For sure, we may be friendlier to morality than Nietzsche is. Nonetheless, in the face of 2,400 years or so of philosophy that wishes to shore up morality against the forces of the self that Nietzsche explores, his work functions as a *necessary corrective*, reminding us of what so much philosophy has wished to avert its eyes from. His is a philosophy of rapture: the key notions, archetypes, and admired individuals of his work—the *Übermensch*, the eternal return of the same, Dionysus, the so-called higher types and the nobles, Napoleon, Goethe, and so on—all work in the service of encouraging a sense of rapture in the face of life and against the enervating forces of morality, which he thought of primarily as hostile to the joy of life. And in encouraging us in this way, Nietzsche wanted to help us hold on to a sense that life is worthwhile after all. What more could one ask of philosophy?

2

Werner Herzog

Human and Animal

Werner Herzog's film *Grizzly Man* (2005) explores the life of Timothy Treadwell, who lived among grizzly bears in Katmai National Park, Alaska, for thirteen summers. He stylized himself as their protector and friend, approaching and in some cases touching them, in defiance of the fact that bears are, of course, potentially extremely dangerous creatures for human beings. Herzog's film utilizes much footage taken by Treadwell of himself and the bears in the course of his summers and thus provides a peculiarly intimate portrait of him, not least as he often spoke directly to the camera, recording his feelings, thoughts, desires, and close contact with the animals.

Among the many fascinating and bizarre moments in the film, one stands out for me. Treadwell is following one of the female bears, whom he has named Wendy. She defecates and moves on. Treadwell then approaches the "poop," as he calls it, and places the open palm of his hand over it, exclaiming in a rapturous outburst that he can feel the heat rising from it. "This was just inside of her! My girl!" he exclaims. He then delicately touches it, exclaiming to the camera: "I know it may seem weird that I touched her poop, but it was inside of her! It's her life! It's her! And she's so precious to me! She gave me Downy! I adore Downy!"

What is so extraordinary about this is that, even without the references to the bear cub, we see immediately the powerful erotic charge that Treadwell expresses in his attitude toward the bear. And it is, furthermore, a moment that might express Herzog's fascination with all those characters—outsiders, misfits, obsessives, and so on—who populate his films and make of his a cinema of rapture. By this I do not mean that most of his characters—whether in his documentaries or in his feature films—are in a state of rapture, for most of them are not, though enough of them are. Nor do I mean that the viewer is always in such a state when watching Herzog's films, still less that Herzog himself is when he makes a film (or otherwise). Rather, I mean that rapture is, so to speak, the *sign* under which his films are made. The body of his work as a whole, that is, expresses the spirit of rapture; this is its style, its "mental atmosphere," to use a phrase of Orwell's. For, as I suggested in the introduction to this book, a life can be lived in the spirit or style of rapture, and so, similarly, I think, a work or a body of work can express a similar style. And part of this is certainly the way in which Herzog goes in search of characters who live at the extremes of human life; this is what these extremes mean in Herzog's work—a vision of life in—or perhaps out of—the spirit of rapture. And these extremes might be of delight or of pain, occasionally bordering on the comic in one of its many possible forms. And it might not always be possible to tell the difference between the delight and the pain.

This is, indeed, so in the case of one of Herzog's films that explicitly calls attention to a kind of rapture, *The Great Ecstasy of the Woodcarver Steiner* (1974). Herzog is actually little interested in the film in the fact that Walter Steiner is a woodcarver. For Steiner is also a ski jumper, and it is this that fascinates him. Indeed, Herzog himself when young harbored the ambition to be a ski jumper but gave up this desire when his best friend was badly injured while jumping. In any case, Steiner is, in fact, a ski flyer, ski flying being a version of ski jumping that involves significantly longer distances. But flying such distances—at that time, 1974, jumps of more than 165 meters were at the outer limits of what could be achieved—is extremely dangerous, and Herzog shows himself fascinated in the film by the sense of danger in jumping such distances, with many shots, shown usually in slow motion, of jumpers who crash. Indeed, very early in the film Herzog shows and then speaks about one of Steiner's crashes in Oberstdorf. Steiner landed at 179 meters, and Herzog is standing and speaking to the camera at just the point where Steiner landed. At this point, says Herzog, ski flying starts to become *unmenschlich*, inhuman. Had Steiner landed 10 meters further, he would have come down on flat ground from a height of 110 meters—and would be dead. Then Herzog says that the point where he is standing, the very place where Steiner had the crash, is the starting point for his film. And although this film was not Herzog's first—he had been making films since 1962—there is nonetheless a sense in which what he says of this film concerning its starting point is also the point of departure for all his films: the place where we see the borders of the human, the place where we arrive at someone or some group of people who, by choice or by the action of luck, good or bad, live at the extreme of what a human being is. And there is something very significant and important in this. For it is, I think, the very nature of what it is to be human to wish to transcend our humanity. Our humanity is marked by a desire to escape it. To be human is to wish to cease being human. By this, I do not mean that each human being, still less each human being all the time, is consciously aware of trying to transcend his or her condition. Rather, I mean that it is a mark of the concept of humanity to wish to transcend our humanity. If you want to know what human beings are, you need to know that this is one of their defining marks, central to their ontological condition.

That may seem terribly abstract. But what I mean can, perhaps, be made clearer by thinking about an example. Human beings are psychologically deeply messy creatures, riven by conflict—conflict between different desires, fantasies, hopes, fears, and so on. We invent ideals, images of a way of life that will put an end to that conflict and allow us to enter into a kind of fullness or plenitude of existence. These ideals may be moral, political, aesthetic, religious, and so on. And the most basic distinction at work here is that between how the world *is*, including how we are, and how the world, how we, *ought to be*. There is no conception of what it is to be human that does not involve this distinction. The need to transcend what we *are* to become what we *ought to be* is central to our self-understanding, even if it is true, as it is, that different individuals experience in themselves the psychological expression of this feature of our ontological condition to different degrees. Our precariously balanced ontological condition has traditionally been expressed by saying that we humans are located between the animals and the angels. The animals and the angels are content in their own condition; they do not long to be other than they are. We are not thus content. And this is why we can look with envy at both animals and angels and long for their way of being sufficient unto themselves, inwardly at peace with themselves. The overarching ideal of Western thought, Christianity, has encouraged us to try to be angels ("Be ye therefore perfect, even as your heavenly Father is perfect" [Matthew 5:48], said Jesus), but, as Montaigne pointed out, if you try to fly like an angel you are likely to sink even lower than you otherwise would have. Montaigne's urbane irony acts as a wonderful antidote to all that, but it is its own ideal, of course, and can itself become another way of seeking to escape from our condition if not handled delicately.

Herzog's interest in the limits or the edges of the human is, then, also an interest in the ordinary or everyday. By looking at the extremes of humanity, he allows us to learn not just about that, but about ourselves as human beings living ordinary, humdrum lives far from the extremes, even as he does not thematize this explicitly. It is as if his films cast a light on the ordinary from the edge: we see the ordinary in this way, but our eyes are still turned toward the extreme. We see what we are by seeing in Herzog's cinema *what we are missing*. Hence it is that his filmmaking shows no interest at all in the stock-in-trade themes of contemporary cinema, most especially the travails of "relationships"—romantic love, marriage, adultery, betrayal, and sex. He scorns our investing so much energy in these matters, the limitedness and narrowness of our vision.

Steiner, to return to him, pushes his humanity to the limit not least because he is willing to risk serious injury or death in pursuit of the moment of rapture as he flies through the air. For it is this sensation of flying that thrills him so deeply. But I do not think that the thrill of flying is only contingently connected with the risks involved. Were he to be able to have the same experience but be guaranteed complete safety—well, it would not be the same experience, not simply in the banal sense that it would not, obviously enough, be dangerous, but in the sense that the danger is central to what that experience is, a necessary component of it. He *wants* the danger. And surely the same must be said of Treadwell. That he could be attacked at any moment by a bear is central to his sense of what he is doing. And, therefore, I think we can say that, although it might seem ghastly that he was, indeed, in the end attacked and eaten by one of the bears—and, of course, in one sense it was— there is nonetheless a way in which it is exactly what he wanted. His death in this way expresses all the bizarre intimacy with the bears that he craved; in a sense he wanted to be wholly at one with them. His death in this way was the price he had to pay for what he wanted, and no other death would have been worthy of him. And while most of us, of course, flee (the risk of) pain and death, we know these nonetheless to be two of the fundamental conditions of our life. In that sense, Steiner and Treadwell live closer to the reality of their humanity than the rest of us do.

► ▷ ►

The notion of liminal humanity comes out forcefully in what is, to my mind, one of Herzog's most perfectly realized films, *The Enigma of Kaspar Hauser* (1974). The title of this film in German is *Jeder für sich und Gott gegen alle*, literally *Each for Himself and God Against All*. That certainly sets the tone for the film, whose main theme is the dreadful *carelessness* of human beings, their unthinking indifference to others, which they often mistake for concern for them. Kaspar, the boy who appeared in Nuremberg in 1828, unable to speak and, as it seemed, never having been in human society, is the hapless victim of this carelessness. When he finally did learn to speak, he said that he had spent the first sixteen years of his life in a *Kellerloch*, a dark basement, receiving his food by an unknown hand while he slept. He is displayed in a kind of circus or freak show, ostensibly to help pay for his upkeep by the local authorities, and is eventually taken in by the philosopher of religion and poet Georg Friedrich Daumer. Lord Stanhope—in reality, Philip Henry Stanhope, 4th Earl Stanhope—visits Kaspar and plans to take him back to England. But nothing comes of the plan, and Kaspar, who had already been attacked once, shortly thereafter succumbs to a second attack and dies.

Herzog's film is not intended to give the exact details of the case, insofar as they are known. His aim is to offer essentially a vision of Kaspar as the good and innocent soul exposed to the degrading influences of a corrupt social world—essentially, a conception of things of roughly Rousseauean provenance. Despite the rather two-dimensional awkwardness of this philosophical background, the film remains one of Herzog's most moving, not least on account of the marvelous screen presence of Bruno S in the central role, the son of a prostitute who had spent some twenty-three years in various institutions and also lived as a busker and a factory worker. He brings to the role an extraordinary gentleness and vulnerability and gives a sense of the tenderness present in human beings if only we would allow ourselves to release it.

Kaspar is, of course, a human being in the biological or genetic sense. No one could doubt that. But Herzog is intent on exploring what it might mean actually to see him as a human being. And it is clear that he wants to suggest that those around Kaspar are—to invoke a notion from the work of Stanley Cavell—soul-blind. With some exceptions—Herr Daumer, for example—those among whom he finds himself cannot see him as having a soul, which we might understand by saying that they cannot see him as the kind of human being for whom things can bear a deep meaning—could, for example, make him despair of his life or think of his life as a gift. He is, for them, a curiosity, not someone with inner depths.

No doubt it is true that, in one way or another, all the great works of art are trying to fathom what it is to be a human being, this "unfinished animal," as Nietzsche put it. But Herzog explicitly thematizes his bafflement in the face of the darkness we confront in looking at ourselves, and this makes him highly unusual among filmmakers. He wants everywhere to discover the humanity in his subjects, even if, as in the case of someone like Treadwell, his presentation of him risks turning him into a mere curiosity, as was Kaspar for those around him.

At the end of *Grizzly Man*, Herzog listens to a recording of Treadwell's last moments. He was with his girlfriend, who, it seems, switched on the camera when the attack by the bear had already begun. But in the panic, the camera fell with the lens cap still on. The tape thus ran to the end, recording the sound but no images. Treadwell's girlfriend was also killed in the attack. Herzog listens to this and is so horrified that he suggests the audio should be destroyed. In a later interview, he describes Treadwell's death as tragic and says that "nobody actually should die like that." But this, I think, misses the point I made earlier, namely, that this death was entirely fitting for Treadwell, gruesome though it certainly was. This is so despite, perhaps even on account of, Herzog's evident pity for Treadwell's dying in the way he did.

Herzog's pity is, I think, better placed in his deeply moving *Land of Silence and Darkness* (1971). This documentary about the deaf-blind follows Fini Straubinger, who lost her sight and hearing early in life, during her teens. Yet it is not for Straubinger that his pity finds its key expression. The film also explores the lives of some of those who are born deaf and blind, now living in a home. One such is Vladimir, who early on had received no support or teaching at all and thus exists in a kind of terrible vegetative state, unable to communicate in any meaningful way. The images are painful to see, and it is as if here we were presented, in the figure of Vladimir, with an image of all possible human ill, all human suffering, utterly without the possibility of the slightest redemption. In search of Vladimir's humanity, the camera reveals it but at the same time submerges it in the surfeit of human suffering, leaving us viewers baffled in the face of own humanity, a humanity we share with Vladimir but, so the camera suggests, only in our intense vulnerability and exposure to a pitiless world. In the case of some of the others in the same home with whom the teachers work, their humanity is revealed by the extraordinary patience and tenderness with which their teachers treat them. This is the kind of film that ought to change one's life forever, shaking one out of one's complacency, but it will not, of course, and this reminds us once again of the terrible carelessness of human beings, of how we live so insouciantly. Man is the ungrateful animal.

The question of pity in Herzog's work has, indeed, not, I think, received as much attention as it might have. It has been overshadowed by his interest in "titanic" personalities, expressed particularly clearly in *Aguirre, the Wrath of God* (1972) and *Fitzcarraldo* (1982), themselves expressive of a life lived in the spirit of rapture: dangerous to themselves and others, massively ambitious. But pity is part of Herzog's style, for it is in many ways the expression of the other side of those titanic personalities that struggle, often to the point of self-destruction, with the natural world and with those who stand in their way or whom they wish to recruit to their own purposes. *Handicapped Future* (1970), for example, is a moving documentary about children born with physical disabilities, in many ways a companion piece to *Land of Silence and Darkness*. The children live together in a special institution, one in which they also come into contact with able-bodied children and can form friendships with them, and it is striking that one of their teachers emphasizes the importance of giving them an education that they might get a career through merit and not out of others' pity. And as she says this, she clearly intimates that they are dependent in the institution on pity, a fact that, it seems, causes her some unease. Or again, Herzog's film version of Büchner's *Woyzeck* (1979) expresses the pity for the eponymous downtrodden soldier that is there in the original play, while his documentary *From One Second to the Next* (2013) about victims and perpetrators of texting while driving conveys pity for the victims of such dangerous stupidity, a pity laced with a quietly humming anger directed toward those responsible for destroying others' lives with such banal thoughtlessness. One of the victims says at the end of the film, in a comment that succinctly expresses the peculiar mindless addiction to which so many of us are prey in using mobile telephones rather than talking face to face: "It's nuts, it's crazy. I don't know why people don't want to talk to each other anyway." There is wisdom in that comment, cutting through as it does the self-congratulatory nonsense we talk in supposing that being able to send text messages—being connected to each other electronically—genuinely enriches our world, and it is hard not to feel that Herzog's film expresses the same thought.

Many have commented on the way in which Herzog's films repeat many of the obsessions of Nietzsche's thinking, but, to my knowledge, no one has made explicit the fact that two poles of his work are pity, on the one hand, and immense self-assertion, on the other, as they are in Nietzsche. And in Nietzsche, the latter often functions as a way of warding off, dampening the effect of, escaping from, the former: in a world so full of suffering, one has to be able to cope with it somehow and, while most of us just ignore it, Nietzsche could not. His attempted response is thus to fantasize an adamantine strength that can bear the sight of it all. Hence all his polemics against pity. And I want to suggest that something similar is going on in Herzog. The ordinary, the everyday, the humdrum are not to be found in his work, as I noted, and while, of course, there may well be many key themes in his films, two of these are certainly, as I said, pity and intense hardness,

53

including a fascination for those whose hardness enables them to trounce over those who might otherwise have merited pity. Both the pity and the hardness are expressions of the unbearability of life, the hardness a kind of *Rausch*, intoxication or rapture, that enables one to go on in the face of it all, the pity a direct response to all that is wrong with life. The tone of rapture that underlies Herzog's work is, then, as in Nietzsche, in large part a matter of a certain latent despair from which he is in flight. One senses this in Nietzsche, even when he is at his most pacific, and it is the same, I think, in Herzog.

If, however, there is after all a middle ground in Herzog, it is a space largely evacuated of any positive meaning. Perhaps what I mean can be seen by considering the scene of the dancing chicken at the end of *Stroszek* (1977): a chicken is enclosed in a miserable plastic and glass box in a tawdry amusement arcade; it has been trained, when coins are inserted into the slot, to press a machine that emits a mind-numbing sound, then overlaid with the sound of a harmonica to which it "dances." This scene gives one a sense of humanity's absolute, implacable desire to do the dirt on life, evacuate it of anything gentle, subtle, decent, generous, or hospitable. This is partly a matter of their treating other animals with such barbarity, as if they were mere fodder to serve the human desire for the lowest kind of entertainment, and partly a matter of the crudity and vulgarity of the whole amusement arcade itself. There is a kind of vision here of human beings as a monstrous, polluting presence in existence. It is a vision of humanity as deserving nothing but contempt. And it seems to me that this vision is present in Herzog's work, lodged somewhere between, and jostling for space with, the pity and

magnificent self-assertion I have mentioned. Again, there
are Nietzschean resonances.

▶ ▷ ▶

Werner Herzog Eats His Shoe (1980) is not a film by Herzog: it is directed by Les Blank, but it is about Herzog, as
the title says, and it has him, indeed, literally eating his
shoe. Herzog had made a bet with—or perhaps, one
should say, offered a challenge to—the filmmaker Errol
Morris: if Morris made a certain documentary film he had
planned, Herzog would eat his shoe. Morris made the film,
and Herzog, no doubt playing up to the public persona he
has carefully constructed over the years, ate his shoe in front
of an audience, having first cooked it in a stock of garlic
and herbs. Les Blank filmed the event.

Morris's film is *Gates of Heaven* (1978). The film, in which
there is no narrator and no one posing any questions, con-
sists of a number of interviews with various individuals
involved with the setting up, or use, of a pet cemetery. Floyd
"Mac" McClure, together with various business associates,
tells of his establishing of the cemetery. It ultimately fails,
and the animals buried there are transferred to another pet
cemetery, Bubbling Well Memorial Park, which is still running at the moment of writing.

The film is a minor masterpiece and amazingly delicately balanced between satire and utter neutrality. Yet
there is no doubt that the film reveals the extraordinary
mawkishness of those involved in the pet cemetery business. Of course, they do not see things this way: for them,
talk of meeting their dead pet dog in an afterlife or of God
greeting a dead pet at the gates of heaven and welcoming it

into paradise, for example, is a sign of genuine and deep love, not cloying sentimentality. And when McClure talks in the same breath of setting up a pet cemetery and of eating steak for dinner without any sense that there is something, at the very least, maladroit in such talk, I feel amazed at his thoughtlessness. Of course, I do not deny that pets can legitimately matter to their owners, and I understand perfectly well that one can feel affection toward a pet, but to hear people speaking in this deeply sentimental way gives me a sense both of total alienation from them, as if they lived in a quite different world from mine and according to a set of values that leave me completely baffled, and yet also of a certain affinity with them, for these people, one feels, must surely be in some way in a state of a certain kind of "quiet desperation," to use Thoreau's phrase, to be able to find such talk and practices consoling. And I know, of course, in my life, such desperation—just not about these things or expressed in these ways.

One might wonder what any of those who speak in Morris's film would make of Timothy Treadwell's attitude toward the bears. Would they see his sentimentality or, since they miss their own, fail to grasp it clearly? I do not know. But there is a way, strange as it may seem to say this, that, for me, these lovers of their pets, in that respect, push at the limits of the human in the kind of way that Treadwell did. In *that* respect: in other ways, this might not be so at all, but in their attitude toward their pets, they seem to me to open a door to a peculiar, baffling affinity with them that, as it were, takes them beyond the human, toward a kind of identity with their animals that seems to me inhuman, as if they might wish to identify themselves so strongly with them—as Treadwell did with the bears—that they lose a sense of their own humanity, precisely in making over their pets so strongly in the image of it.

In Blank's film, in any case, Herzog comments that Morris's film tells one more about the United States than the annual State of the Union Address and, clearly understanding the film as I have done, says that it is a film about the loss of emotions and the distortion and degeneration of feelings. It is, he says, a very sad film. But he also makes the point that the film is dealing with what happens to emotions such as love in late capitalism. His idea, I take it, is that the sentimentality of these pet owners is a product or expression of the world in which we live, its spiritual emptiness and banality. But this, interestingly enough, was just the thing that Treadwell thought he was trying to escape, so, oddly enough, it looks from the present point of view that he is as much an expression of decadent capitalism's hollowness as those who long to join their pets in heaven. The shallowness of late capitalism is, we might say, a specific form of rapture in which we can lose ourselves through sentimentality. And if Oscar Wilde is right that sentimentality is the Bank Holiday of cynicism, it perhaps becomes less surprising that so many of our cultural products are pitched between sentimentality and violence, both forms of rapture of a degraded, cheapened, easily available kind.

I said earlier that the ordinary and quotidian is absent from Herzog's filmmaking. His is a cinema relentlessly hostile to the bourgeois values of fitting seamlessly into the bureaucratic machinery governing our lives through instrumental rationality, with all that this demands by way of hypocrisy and a focus on comfort and order. Hence it is that when Herzog is directly concerned with the capitalist world, this is usually only insofar as he can condemn it, as in *Glaube und Währung* (*God's Angry Man*; more literally: *Faith and Currency*, 1981), a documentary about Gene Scott, a televangelist with his own television and business empire, an empire itself enmeshed in various legal actions on account of Scott's suspect financial practices. Herzog's main focus is on Scott's ability to persuade his audience to part with hundreds of thousands of dollars to his benefit, or the benefit of his church, as he claims, but he is clearly interested not simply in this man's avarice but also in the fact that the capitalist system can throw up such a figure, one who can move frictionlessly between talk of God and Jesus, on the one hand, and expressions of greed that are almost admirable in their audacious refutation of everything that Jesus stood for, on the other. In Woody Allen's *Hannah and Her Sisters* (1986), Frederick (Max von Sydow) remarks that, if Jesus came back and saw what was going on in his name, he would never stop throwing up—and it is the TV evangelists whom he has in mind. It is completely obvious that Herzog shares the sentiment. But I take it that Herzog means his criticism to be one that strikes all of us in our bourgeois comfort, including those of us who share his view of Scott: the evangelist is representative of a whole culture from which we benefit, and the problem cannot be solved by tinkering with the details. What is needed is a root and branch clear out, and this is why Herzog continues to be fascinated by those human beings who push at the limits of the humanity, for they represent hope: they have, so to speak, at least from the point of view of Herzog's myth-making perspective, carried out the clear out on themselves, or found that it has been carried out on them by their ejection from bourgeois complacency. And once again sentimentality is to the fore in Herzog's extended interview with Scott in which he claims that the only thing he really wants is to get away from his life as he now lives it: this enables him to stylize himself in his own self-image as a martyr for the cause, all the while enjoying the comforts provided by a material life of enormous ease.

Herzog's attitude toward religion is distinctly ambivalent. For there is, after all, a grudging admiration for a figure like Scott in his work, if only because, whatever else he is, he is *interesting*. At one point he rants at the camera as he seeks to cajole his viewers to cough up just $600 dollars more to reach takings of a sum total of $23,000 for the day. He is beside himself with anger as he yells at those watching him at home. Somehow one feels a kind of esteem for the sheer nerve of the thing: that he could have thought of doing anything so utterly ludicrous in the name of Christianity makes of him a fascinating figure. That we are to feel this way is evidently Herzog's aim.

Still, the naked capitalism of Scott's tirade—indeed, of his whole way of life—is in the end for Herzog less interesting than what he labels as one of its other peculiar products, the strange language that cattle auctioneers have developed and which he charts in *How Much Wood Would a Woodchuck Chuck* (1976), a documentary film that records the World Livestock Auctioneer Championship in New Holland, Pennsylvania. The film is subtitled *Observations on a New Language* (*Beobachtungen zu einer neuen Sprache*), and Herzog is clearly fascinated by the way in which the process of buying and selling has led to the development of the language used by the auctioneers, stock phrases spoken so quickly that no one untrained in the technique can really understand what is being said, the language sounding for all the world like a kind of ritual, almost sung or chanted incantation. There is almost a redemptive quality in this language, redemptive, that is, of the utilitarian aims of buying and selling. And there is a marvelous foil to the auction in the fact that it takes place in Lancaster County, which has a large Amish population, whose pacifism and rejection of modern technology stand in sharp contrast to the spirit of commercial haggling, barter, and negotiation. Herzog at no point directly suggests the superiority of the Amish way of life over that of the auctioneers, and it is not, I think, his intention to do so. But he seems, nonetheless, to respect the quiet nobility and simplicity of their way of being, a point that is reinforced in the later *From One Second to the Next*, to which I have already referred, in which we see an interview with one Chandler Gerber, who, while driving and texting, rammed into an Amish family in their buggy on the road in front of him, killing two children and a teenager. Gerber reads out a letter he later received from Martin Schwartz, the father of the children, in which Schwartz offers forgiveness to him and says he trusts in God.

Religion, indeed, interests Herzog for its capacity to enchant the world, as we see clearly *Bells from the Deep* (1993), a film about faith and superstition in Russia. But in a way one might be able to say this about all the subjects of his films. He is fascinated by the endless variety that human life can take and goes everywhere in search of "exotic specimens." He is a kind of anthropologist, driven to travel in search of the outrageous and outlandish, and perhaps he too at times finds a kind of rapturous delight in this restlessness.

▶ ▷ ▶

Early in this chapter I mentioned the woodcarver Steiner as a kind of paradigm case of rapture in Herzog's films. The idea of flight is important here, and I wish to end by saying something about one other film of Herzog's in which the rapture of flight figures centrally.

This is *Little Dieter Needs to Fly* (1997). Dieter Dengler, who was born in Germany but emigrated to the United States, had just one burning desire: to fly. He became a U.S. Navy aviator and was shot down in 1966 over Laos in the early phase of the Vietnam War. He was taken prisoner and was tortured, but he managed to escape, spending twenty-three days on the run in the jungle, finally being rescued in a state of abject physical and mental suffering—his weight was under 49 kilos (85 pounds).

Dengler describes how he conceived the longing to fly. He grew up in Wildberg, a town in the Schwarzwald, during the Second World War, and, on one occasion, enemy airplanes were engaged over his town: one of them passed right in front of his house as he and his brother looked out; he could see the pilot; and one of the plane's wings passed within feet of his house as the pilot rose and banked. It was, he said, as if an almighty being had come down. In that moment, says Dengler, he knew one thing: he needed to fly, and it is clear that the longing for absolute freedom in flight was key to this need. As this was not possible in postwar Germany, he went to the United States. He had had, of course, no intention at all to get caught up in a war.

He spent the rest of his life haunted by his ordeal.

Like Steiner, Dengler saw in flying a moment of complete freedom, and he continued to fly after the war, becoming a test pilot. At times the only place he could sleep was the cockpit of a fighter plane: only here did he feel safe. Steiner, we remember, when he made his exceptionally long jump, narrowly escaped death. So did Dengler when he was shot down from the skies. He tells us that, when he escaped and was making his way through the jungle, he was with his fellow escapee and friend Duane Martin. Martin was hacked to death with a machete by a villager in one of the places where they had sought to steal some food. Dengler managed to get away and thereafter was accompanied in the jungle only by a large bear that was circling him, waiting for him to die so that it could eat him. Dengler remarks that this bear was then his only friend; his only friend was death. Yet death spurned him and he survived.

In their different ways, Steiner and Dengler push themselves to the limits of what they are as human beings in pursuit of a moment of total freedom. This is their rapture: a loss of self in a condition of total liberation from constraint. Yet both, in longing for and achieving this, risked a loss of self even greater: that of death. Herzog's filmmaking says to us: life lived close to death is a rapturous loss of self. But if you live like this, you must be prepared for a loss of self that is not so much rapturous as, rather, total extinction.

3

Pierre Bonnard

Desire and Skepticism

Last year I was in Paris for a few days and spent several hours one morning in the Musée d'Orsay. I was particularly keen to see again the paintings of Pierre Bonnard, but, though I know his work well, I was amazed by one in particular: *Nu accroupi au tub* (1918). And the staggering thing about this painting, to my mind, the thing that left me amazed, was not so much the nude herself as the rendering of the water that the woman pours from the jug held in her right hand into the tub in which she will wash herself. The sensation of movement that comes from the water, that is *in* the water, that *is* the water, is overwhelming. I stood lost to myself and the world in a rapture of delight that anyone can paint anything so simple yet so profound, so utterly commonplace, yet so lifted from the everyday.

► ▷ ►

I cannot remember when I first encountered the paintings of Bonnard, but it was probably about thirty years ago. He was less fashionable then than now, so I am not sure how I discovered him, but, when I did, I immediately felt deeply drawn to him. When one thinks about the artists, novelists, poets, and so on to whom one finds oneself most deeply attracted, whose work one finds resonates deeply with one, there can be a certain sense of mystery, a feeling that something is taking hold of one for reasons that one cannot fully fathom. These reasons may become a little less obscure later. In my case, I sense that Bonnard struck me with such force, and continues to do so, for reasons deeply connected with the peculiar emotional and material poverty of my childhood, a period in my life characterized by a feeling, for me, that all of life was squalid and compromised, tainted by the presence of violence, lies, and manipulation. Here in Bonnard one finds the antithesis of all that—and I am thinking here in the first instance of his paintings of gardens, hills, woods: light, color, open windows, warm air, sunshine, a sense that life can be unforced, does not need to be relentlessly pressured, can be lived in a spirit of ease and gentle generosity. When I see Bonnard's canvases, I have the sense that *this* is how life should be lived, that *here* is vision fit for human beings, perhaps especially for those human beings who, like me, cannot remember a moment when they were not troubled by life. Here is a plenitude, not one informed by weariness, but by a sense of arrival, that this was what all the struggles were for, something redemptive and complete, where the mind can rest with itself.

Michel Serres, discussing Bonnard's *Le peignoir* (c. 1890), also in the Musée d'Orsay, says that it appeals as much to the sense of touch as to that of sight.[1] This is owing to Bonnard's way of leaving parts of the canvas exposed and untreated, and to his application of tissue as well as paint to the canvas. This is a deeply arresting thought. We normally suppose that paintings appeal only to the eye, as we think that music appeals only to the ear. But haptic paintings, such as this one by Bonnard, overflow themselves, so to speak, and appeal to the sense of touch as well as to that of sight. Yet I suppose that we imagine that, if this is so, then it is a matter of what we might experience if we were to touch the canvas, and this is what Serres seems to be saying: we engage imaginatively in such an act in front of the painting. But my sense of the tactile quality of Bonnard's paintings goes beyond that. The rapture I feel in front of his canvases of landscapes is that of feeling this light, these colors, on the skin of my body: not touching, but being touched. This, as I have said, is the experience of Bonnard's landscapes and gardens: I am not *in front of* the paintings after all but *inside* them, caressed by them, held in safety by the places they are, my body nurtured and nourished by the warmth, light, and color.

My sense of Bonnard and what he means to me could be read as a failing on my part. John Berger is right when he says of Bonnard: "There is very little of the post-1914 world in Bonnard's work. There is very little to disturb— except perhaps the unnatural peacefulness of it all. His art is intimate, contemplative, privileged, secluded. It is an art about cultivating one's own garden." Berger thus reads the appeal of Bonnard in part in terms of a retreat from "political realities and confidence." He sees the landscapes and the related paintings—of meals and still lifes, for example— as not facing up to the difficulties of the world. Tragedy is not here confronted and, as it may be, incorporated or acknowledged; it is simply avoided. He says: "The trouble

65

with the landscapes and still lifes and meals—the weakness expressed through their colour—is that in them the surrounding world conflicts are . . . ignored."[2]

It is not clear what one is to make of this criticism, for so much depends on context. What exactly is the "trouble"? Presumably, Berger cannot be intending to suggest that it would be better were Bonnard's vision of the world, as expressed in these paintings, not to exist. It could hardly be supposed that the world would be richer or deeper were it absent; there are such visions, visions we would be better off without, but this is not one of them. Is the worry then that it is partial? Or too partial, since no vision of life could capture the whole of life? Might someone mistake the partial for the complete? Perhaps—and I shall return to this—but my love for this vision of life contains no such mistake. I am well aware that it is a limited vision. Indeed, that awareness is precisely one reason why I find it can offer so much: it does so because I know that it offers but a temporary sense of release, of ease, of delight.

Perhaps what is at issue here is in part a matter of when or how one comes to find Bonnard's vision so arresting, so resonant. For Berger talks as if the problem—the trouble—might be that one may be, so to speak, *helpless* in the face of Bonnard's idea of cultivating one's own garden, bewitched by it, so that one would be prey to a kind of irresponsibility, one that ignored the difficulties of the world, including its political problems. But one is not so helpless. One comes to it having, so to speak, passed through some of the world's difficulties, so one is perfectly capable of seeing it for what it is while *also* losing oneself in it. One can *place* it.

But might there after all be someone who is helpless in the way Berger seems to have in mind? Yes, no doubt.

66

Someone might have a vision of life whose center is given by what Bonnard offers in these paintings—a certain kind of quietism, let us say. But is that so terrible? It is not obvious why. For sure, not everyone could be like this (and not everyone will ever be like this). But that is neither here nor there. I might be delighted by another in his quietism: as D. H. Lawrence would have said, it takes his sort to make all sorts.

But perhaps what Berger is really worried about is that one might not be able to see that a certain vision is limited. Here he certainly has a point. This, I think, regularly happens in—to take a quite different example—the case of Nietzsche. What I mean is this: when one reads Nietzsche, one can be completely overwhelmed, caught up, say, in his sense that slave morality dominates the contemporary ethical scene, that modern morality has made a fetish out of pity, that people have become like tame farmyard animals, lacking an edge and self-assertion, that we live on an "ascetic planet," that *ressentiment* is the motor of morality, and so on. There are countless books on Nietzsche that talk of him as if these kinds of claims are correct, more or less so anyway, or seek to show that they are. But this is Nietzsche's way of bewitching us. If we raise our eyes from his texts and look at the world at his time with its wars, conflicts, violence, abject poverty, rampant disease, appalling lack of basic hygiene for millions . . . can we really believe that a central moral problem was the presence of too great a valuation of pity, that slave morality had come to dominate Europe, and so on? For sure, Nietzsche has helped us see better where *ressentiment* is operative, and we would have missed much of this without him, but greed, envy, vanity, spitefulness, and much else besides also cloak

themselves readily in the trappings of morality and provide its motive force—not that Nietzsche denies this, on
the contrary, but he hardly explores it with the kind of attention he devotes to *ressentiment*. The truth is that Nietzsche's
view here is both profoundly limited and pitched at such a
high level of abstraction—he himself sees this when he
says, for example, that the Earth would appear to be an
ascetic planet from a distant star—that it is hard to see
how it connects with the ins and outs of quotidian existence,
and, although it may help us to see some things with
extreme clarity and insight for the first time, it will conceal
many more from us. There is in Nietzsche the relentless-
ness of a singular vision that means he obscures much
from view and *takes us in*. He does so in part through the
brilliance of his prose and in part because, when one reads
Nietzsche for the first time, one senses immediately that
one has never read anyone before with such a voice: it is
unparalleled. He does everything he can to stop us from
looking over the edge of his thinking when we are exploring it, and the truth is that he is largely successful in doing
so. Hence it is that two common reactions to Nietzsche are
more or less total rejection, on the one hand, or reading of
him in his own terms, on the other. This is what makes
reading Nietzsche so hard—trying to get the right critical
distance from him so that one can take him fully seriously
and yet not be bamboozled or browbeaten. But I am glad
that Nietzsche lived, despite, or perhaps because of, the
strange yet powerful way in which his thinking is like a
scalpel, incisive and capable of immense penetration,
though lacking (it might seem odd to say this of him, but it
is true) in breadth and a capacious understanding of human
affairs. Yet had he been my friend, I would have tried, out

of my love for him, to help him live with just a little more of what Bonnard has to offer—less like a vivisectionist (to use an image he uses of others in criticism, but which applies to him), and more like a gardener. He knew, in the end, and not just in the end, that he needed it: hence his obsession with Adalbert Stifter's *Nachsommer*, a novel that might have been written, indeed, in Bonnard's garden in order to reflect its delights, or his comments later on Bizet as an antidote to Wagner.

Berger, I noted, claims that it is through Bonnard's colors that we see the weakness of the landscapes and so on, and he compares the use of these colors here with their use in the numerous nudes he painted of his model Marthe de Méligny, who was his lover and then wife. He writes:

> The typical mature Bonnard bias of colour—towards marble whites, magenta, pale cadmium yellow, ceramic blues, terracotta reds, silver greys, stained purple, all unified like reflections on the inside of an oyster—this bias tends in the landscapes to make them look mythical, even faery; in the still lifes it tends to give the fruit or the glasses or the napkins a silken glamour, as though they were part of a legendary tapestry woven from threads whose colours are too intense, too glossy; but in the nudes the same bias seems only to add conviction.[3]

This is, of course, fine criticism, and Berger is a very fine observer, without a doubt. And it is certainly true that he is right that some of the landscapes look mythical in a damaging way: *La Symphonie pastorale* (1916/1920), also in the Musée d'Orsay, is an example. It is also so of the decorative panels that he painted for Misia Godebska in 1906. But the problems here seem to me to have more to do with subject matter and composition than with color, and Berger's generalization seems gratuitous. I suspect that he was searching for something in the paintings in order to ground his objection to their apolitical rejection of the modernity, but it would have been cleaner and more direct to object to the vision as such than make the detour through reflection on Bonnard's colors. This suspicion is only strengthened by noting that the nudes are no less apolitical than the landscapes, but that Berger was profoundly sensitive to, and ready to embrace, representations of those moments of intimate physical love that turn their back on the political. Here, in this intimacy between us, he seems to say, we can leave the political behind for a moment for the profound love we have for each other; but when the moment is past and we must again look out of the window at the world, here we must face the political. Yet Bonnard carries over, as it were, that moment of shared physical love into the outside world. It is to this, I think, that Berger really objects. The objection, as I have suggested, would carry weight if one supposed that this was all the outside world was; but it is not necessary to follow Berger in his reflections here.

Berger, in any case, finds the nudes convincing. Why? The key point in his interpretation is to note—and this is certainly true in many of the canvases—the way in which Marthe is so often represented as overflowing the space of her own body: the lines of paint demarcating the external limits of her body are often hard to discern and her body flows away into the water in which she is lying, or the light in which she is recumbent and so on. As Berger puts it: "Her image emanates outwards from her until she is to be found everywhere except within the limits of her physical presence."[4] Now this, says Berger, is a visual representation of the experience of the "crystallisation" of love, as Stendhal so famously described it. If you love a woman, says Stendhal,

> you take pleasure in endowing her with a thousand perfections.... In the end you overrate her as utterly magnificent, as something fallen from Heaven, whom you do not know but is sure to be yours.
> If you leave a lover with his thoughts for twenty-four hours, this is what you will find.
> At the salt mines of Salzburg they throw a small, leafless wintry branch into the depths of the abandoned excavation. Two or three months later they pull it out covered with a shining deposit of crystals. The smallest twigs, no bigger than the claw of a titmouse, are studded with an infinity of dazzling and shimmering diamonds. The original branch can no longer be recognised.
> What I call crystallisation is a process of the mind which draws from everything that occurs new proofs that the loved one is perfect.[5]

Berger's point about Bonnard's paintings of Marthe, if I have understood him correctly, is that her overflowing of her own physical space, of the limits of her own body, gives a sense of accretion and addition to her of the kind that Stendhal means to evoke in speaking of the branch now covered in the sparkling diamonds. Hence Berger writes:

> Many other painters have of course idealized women whom they have painted. But straightforward idealization becomes in effect indistinguishable from flattery or pure

71

fantasy. It is no way does justice to the energy involved in the psychological state of being in love. What makes Bonnard's contribution unique is the way that he shows in pictorial terms how the image of the beloved emanates *outwards from her* with such dominance that finally her actual physical presence becomes curiously incidental and in itself indefinable. (If it could be defined, it would become banal.)[6]

So we *see* Bonnard's love for Marthe in these paintings in her overflowing of her own physical limits and space.

Here, then, we see why Berger thinks that Bonnard's nudes face the tragedy of human life: Marthe is here only half present and yet is wholly loved. This *is* the tragedy of this kind of love. And although Berger does not say this, I imagine he had this in mind: the person we love is never really or fully known to us and, to the extent that he or she is, will be understood as the frail, weak, vulnerable creature he or she really is, inescapably shabby as we all are, and we cannot say that he or she merits or deserves our love. ("Use every man after his desert, and who should 'scape whipping?" asked Hamlet.) But we love nonetheless. Contrary to the Christian tradition that tells us we see someone most clearly when we love him or her, the truth is the opposite: we always love gratuitously, beyond merit, beyond what the other is, and this is its beauty *and* its tragedy, its beauty *because* it is tragic. The fact that Marthe may in some literal sense only have been half present to Bonnard, since she may well have been neurasthenic, and was obsessed with washing and bathing, only adds a personal dimension to the universal truth, as Berger notes.

The rapture of Bonnard's canvases is then, perhaps, that of being in love. And this goes too, I think, for the landscapes, which are, as I suggested, continuations of the moment of physical love intimated by the nudes. This is a world bathed in physical love, its tenderness and generosity—this gift that we can give to one another.

But here "physical love" should not be thought of only in terms of the act of love itself. Rather, what is at stake is a kind of erotics of the world, one example of which is the act of physical love. What we have in Bonnard is the world as erotic. And what I mean by this is perhaps best expressed by my availing myself here of some thoughts from Merleau-Ponty, specifically the chapter in his *The Phenomenology of Perception* entitled "The Body in Its Sexual Being."

Merleau-Ponty's philosophically lyrical approach resists, I think, adequate paraphrase and demands that the reader allow himself or herself to be *moved* by his sense, evident here as elsewhere in his work, of what one might call the magnificent plenitude of human life, more particularly, the plenitude of the embodied human being in his relations with the material world, his, so to speak, *leaning into it* with a kind of hunger for experience. In any case, what Merleau-Ponty wishes to explore in the chapter in question is our affective life, by which he clearly means, roughly speaking, the fact that things *matter* to us in various ways. This is why he proposes to speak of desire or love. And a key point in his thinking is that the world matters to us in various ways, not because we survey it neutrally, as it were, registering its properties as to their capacity, say, to provide pleasure or pain, but because we are constantly *projecting* ourselves into the world. We are beings who care about the world, and we do so because we are embodied or, rather, because we are thinking, experiencing, and—crucially— *acting* bodies, giving ourselves over to the world, and taking that world into us, in way that resists an understanding of ourselves as being subject to "a mosaic of affective states . . . each sealed within itself."[7] I act on the ground of my whole embodied being, and my caring about this or that expresses my projected being, my being-toward-the-world—for example, comporting myself toward this situation as one of sexual interest or that situation as one of convivial sharing of a meal or some other situation as one of intense intellectual activity. Things rise up for me in the world on the basis of these forms of comportment, not the other way round, as if I were to "put together" the individual things I am doing only to discover, so to speak, that I am, say, engaged in an act of religious worship or family celebration or teaching a class.

Merleau-Ponty, I noted, started by thinking of the notion of desire or love. He means these as two synonymous terms for expressing our *embodied leaning into the world*. And he seems to be taking sexual desire as the paradigm expression of this, a kind of primordial image of desire as such, just a Freud did, and others too—Keats, for example. This does not mean that he is claiming that we are always in a state of sexual desire or arousal, of course, or anything silly like that, but rather this:

> From the part of the body which it especially occupies, sexuality spreads forth like an odour or a sound. . . . Taken in this way, as an ambiguous atmosphere, sexuality is co-extensive with life. In other words, ambiguity is of the

essence of human existence, and everything we live or think has always several meanings. . . . There is interfusion between sexuality and existence, which means that existence permeates sexuality and *vice versa*, so that it is impossible to determine, in a given decision or action, the proportion of sexual to other motivations, impossible to label a decision or act "sexual" or "non-sexual."[8]

It seems that the idea of ambiguity is key here, again making sexual desire primordially central for understanding human beings as embodied, desiring creatures, since there is a very specific ambiguity in sexuality, as the body of each lover is an active, appropriating body for him or her but also passive, a desired object for the other lover. The ambiguity of human life is mirrored in the ambiguity of sexual desire, and human life *is* ambiguous because sexual desire is ambiguous.

So now we can see better what I meant by saying that in Bonnard we have an erotics of the world. I could put my thought this way: if you want to know what Merleau-Ponty means in his claims about sexuality, if you want a representation of it, it is there in Bonnard's canvases. Bonnard *shows* us what Merleau-Ponty means. His world is a world in which everything is both sexual and nonsexual, in which everything is both and neither. To give oneself up to Bonnard's canvases is to give oneself up to an experience in which one has raised to consciousness, or rather to embodied awareness, raised to *feeling*, what Merleau-Ponty says is the case all the time, but which we do not notice, since we just *live it* or *are lived by it*. Here, we *feel* it.

▶ ▷ ▶

As I remarked earlier, there is often something mysterious about the way in which an artist or writer or the like appeals to one. Part of what is at issue here, I think, is the moment in one's life when one comes across the work in question. Stefan Zweig, for example, begins his essay on Montaigne thus:

> There are just a few writers who are accessible to anyone at any age or stage of life—Homer, Shakespeare, Goethe, Balzac, Tolstoy—and then again there are others whose meaning is revealed only at a specific moment. Montaigne is one of these. In order to acknowledge his real worth, one should not be too young or too deprived of experience and disappointment, and his free and unswerving thinking will be most helpful to such a generation as ours, thrown by fate into the cataract of the world's turmoil. Only the person whose soul is in turmoil as a result of life in an epoch where war, violence and ideological tyranny threaten the individual's life, together with the most precious substance in that life, individual freedom, can know how much courage, how much sincerity and resolve are required to remain faithful to his inner self in these times of the herd's madness. . . . Only someone who has tested himself can appreciate Montaigne's wisdom and greatness.[9]

Zweig was writing this in 1941/1942, and it is hardly surprising that he emphasizes the condition of his generation in his remarks. But even those of us lucky enough to live in one of the few pockets of peace in this agitated world so ill at ease with itself can see exactly what he means: Montaigne speaks especially to those troubled by life, and by, say, middle age, most people have had to confront both the world and themselves enough to appreciate the force of Montaigne's writing, if they are willing and able to make space for it in their life.

I discovered Bonnard when I was young, but I think, nonetheless, that he is the kind of painter most likely to be appreciated by those who have found themselves disappointed by life. The reason for this is that his vision of a loving cultivation of one's garden is not likely to appeal to youth. For, as Joseph Conrad remarked in *Lord Jim*: "Youth is insolent; it is its right—its necessity; it has got to assert itself, and all assertion in this world of doubts is a defiance, is an insolence."[10] The insolence of youth is at odds with the gentle skepticism of Bonnard's vision, and it belongs to youth, not in the sense that age or old age does not have it, but in the sense that youth has it as its *right*, as Conrad says. "It is the nature of youth not to want the counsel of gentleness, of scepticism," says Zweig.[11] What we know as we get older is that the world will continue on its metaled ways even if we can effect *local* changes for the better. It is Hamlet's vision that the time is out of joint and that nothing can change that. The human condition—its blindness, its carelessness—remains what it is, and all one can do is attend to one's own blindness, one's own carelessness, in the hope that doing so may, as I say, effect some local change for the better. Bonnard bids us to love a little better here and now, in the intimacy of our lives. For he knows that one of the hardest things to do is to love those close to us, and that we often deceive ourselves into supposing we love them well when, in fact, what we are doing is ignoring them and focusing on some distant good that seems so much grander. Bonnard is not just in love with Marthe; he loves her. And his endless canvases of her are attempts to understand that love, to be equal to it, to be worthy of it. We think we can love those close to us and then, so to speak, get on with our lives. We miss the truth that loving those close to us is an endless task, that we have to shake ourselves each day to be reminded of it, to shake ourselves to wake from our complacency, and Bonnard's paintings of Marthe are his way of shaking himself.

Conrad said that "all assertion in this world of doubts is a defiance, is an insolence." This has to be understood aright. He does not mean that we should not say what we think or seek to show why we are right. Nor does he mean that there are not some views, some ways of looking at the world, some ways of treating each other, that are simply beyond the pale—forms of indifference, cruelty, or barbarity. He means, rather, that we need to be attentive as much to the spirit in which we believe what we believe as to what we believe itself, the content, so to speak. There is nothing in the human condition so common as for us to suppose we know better than others, see more clearly than they do, have greater insight. As Cioran pointed out, we are all incipiently fanatics. Conrad's comment is a *corrective* to our being as Cioran says we are, and it is a reminder of the fool we each carry around with us, the fool that each of us is. We constantly need to be reminded that we do not know, that we are all of us confused, that assertions of certainty are virtually always forms of defensiveness for our own unclarities, blindness, weakness, and vulnerability. Conrad is recommending the spirit of skepticism even when we claim to know or be certain, a way of holding our beliefs that leaves them open, porous, generous.

Bonnard is not the greatest of painters, nor even the greatest of painters in the twentieth century. There is no doubt, as I have said, that his vision is in some ways narrow or limited. But, in the warmth of his colors, in his vision of the world as an object of love, in his erotics of the world he says to us: stop asserting anything at all for this moment and just *look and feel*. He returns us to our body and, in doing so, delivers us up to the world—and the world to us.

4

Reverie

Gardening and the Material World

O nce a year, I spend a week at a small meditation center in the west of England. Most of the week is spent
in silence and is occupied—apart from the meditation,
of course—with gardening and the preparing and cooking of food for the small community of people—nine
other retreatants and two "coordinators"—who are there
for the week.

I started going to the retreat in the wake of a period of
intense melancholy, almost certainly related to my mother's death, and poor physical health. I felt *distracted* from
much that matters to me in life, and this was both cause
and effect of my melancholy, though not, of course, the
only cause or effect, tiredness also playing a significant
role here, the result, no doubt, of a life focused too much
on work and learning and pushing myself intellectually and
physically, and too little on simply looking and being. Around
the same time I started to explore various body-based ther-
apies, such as cranial-sacral therapy and sophrology, aware
that I needed to slow down and be more attentive to the

body's subtle needs, instead of always pushing it to give more, as I have always done, for example, in long-distance running. One person whom I consulted around this time advised me to "dream" more—she wrote in her notes of advice for me at the end of my session with her: "*s'accorder 'du rêve'* ": "allow oneself to dream." I understood her to be advising me to do what I was beginning to explore anyway in trying to pay attention to how I was living my life, but I think she also meant that I should literally daydream more: be idle, relax, say, in a pool of sunlight like a cat, and allow my mind to wander. Temperamentally, I find this very hard—I have always been a very driven person—and my training as a philosopher hardly helped me in this regard, since philosophy is in many ways very bad at nourishing the imagination, accepting flights of fancy, of fantasy. I have always found this side of philosophy objectionable and unhelpful for both intellectual and temperamental reasons.

Between September 9 and October 25, 1765, Jean-Jacques Rousseau spent a few weeks on St. Peter's Island in Lake Biel in the canton of Bern, Switzerland. He describes the stay in the fifth of his *Les rêveries du promeneur solitaire* (*Reveries of the Solitary Walker*). I know of no text that better captures the rapture of a week of silent meditation and gardening—though in the strictest sense he was neither meditating nor gardening.

Rousseau had gone to the island to seek tranquility after a number of acts of hostility against him, including the seizure by the authorities in Switzerland of copies of the *Contrat social* and *Émile*, and the lapidation of his house. He sought tranquility, and this is what he found, along with what by his own account was the most rapturous moment of his life.

On the island—which, he says, was known in Neuchâtel as "La Motte"—he concentrated on himself, withdrew into his inner self. But this has to be understood aright, for he certainly does not mean that he did not pay attention to his surroundings. Quite the contrary, for he was, for example, intensely interested in the flora and fauna of the island. What he means is, rather, that, just as Montaigne said of himself when he retreated to his tower to concentrate on himself, he aimed to achieve—and did achieve—a way of simply letting himself be who he was, fully aware of himself, for the things in the external world to which he paid attention allowed him to do this: they did not assail or trouble or impose themselves on him. They did not, in the negative sense, distract him, that is, distract him in the way that so much in human life does, by cluttering up the mind with useless thoughts and feelings, preventing one from focusing on what one really cares about, the result of which is always a feeling of pointlessly wasted energy, of frenetic and unfocused activity, and of emptiness and ash in the mouth. Here he was able, he tells us, to be one of those who like "to drink deeply [s'enivrer à loisir] the beauty of nature and to meditate [se recueillir] in a silence broken by no other sound than the cry of eagles, the occasional warbling of birds, and the roar of streams cascading down the mountains."[1] Absolutely crucial in Rousseau's account of his happiness on the island—and he means by happiness the "gentle rapture" (les douces extases) his time on the island gave him—is his sense that there was a solidity to his state there. Picking up on the stream of French thought running from at least Montaigne, through Pascal and the moralistes such as La Rochefoucauld, up to his reflections, he notes that we spend most of our life in the past or the

83

future, actuated, on the one hand, by nostalgia or regret and, on the other, by hope, usually for things that never come to pass anyway and, if they do, not in the form we wish—that is, to a greater or lesser (usually greater) extent as a disappointment. In this "continual earthly flux," as he puts it, happiness is usually given to us in the form of fleeting moments, and "how can one call a fleeting state happiness when it leaves our heart anxious and empty, regretting something past or desiring something else later?"[2] But on La Motte, Rousseau experienced a different kind of happiness.

What Rousseau possessed on St. Peter's Island was what we now call mindfulness:

> What does one possess [De quoi jouit-on] in such a situation? Nothing external to oneself, nothing but oneself and one's own existence; as long as this state lasts one is sufficient unto oneself like God. The feeling of existence stripped of every other emotion is by itself a precious feeling of contentment and of peace, which alone would suffice to make this existence cherished and gentle to whoever knew how to put at a distance all the mundane and sensual impressions that ceaselessly distract us from, and disturb, our pleasure [douceur] here below.[3]

It is exactly this state that is the meditative state: one is in a state of heightened awareness of oneself and untroubled; yet the world is there, present to consciousness as it is *now*.

Again and again, Rousseau tells us that here he "sensed with pleasure [his] being [*existence*]" and that he gave himself up to idleness (though nothing in English can quite capture the sense of delicious ease captured in the French word *oisiveté*), losing himself in daydreams (*plongé dans milles rêveries confuses mais délicieuses*) as he lay on a hilltop or at the water's edge or in a boat on the lake, drifting around as the current might desire. But, again, he has to be understood aright since he also spent many mornings in search of the countless varieties of plants on the island, studying them with the aid of a magnifying glass and Linnaeus's *Systema Naturae*. Rousseau experienced both himself *and* the world in their plenitude.

In all this, Rousseau stresses, his delight was in part owing to his being left alone by the outside world. He even left his books in the trunk in which they arrived, and his only company was afforded by a steward of the island and his family, as well as his lover Thérèse Levasseur.

It is, of course, not incidental that Rousseau was where he was. The island was deeply conducive to his meditative state. I think it would be fair to say that we could think of the island as a garden. As Robert Pogue Harrison says in his *Gardens: An Essay on the Human Condition*: "In Western culture it has been the garden, whether real or imaginary, that has provided sanctuary from the frenzy and tumult of history."[4] For sure, this does not mean that only gardens can provide such sanctuary. But given the features of the St. Peter's Island as Rousseau describes them, and given also that he was most certainly seeking sanctuary, I think it is fair to say that it was as a garden that it entered into his imagination.

Harrison discusses in one of his chapters the book *The Gardener's Year* by the Czech writer Karel Čapek, and he quotes Verlyn Klinkenborg from his introduction to the book: "Most students of Čapek believe gardening is a subset of life, whereas gardeners, including Čapek, understand that life is a subset of gardening."[5] I take it that this means that, for the gardener, the world is seen in the light of what the garden is and what it is to work in a garden. There are many aspects to this, no doubt, but for my purposes, in the context of Rousseau, I think the key thing is the light that his time on La Motte casts on the world, what it teaches him—and us—about life. There are, I think, two issues here.

The first, most obvious point in this regard to which Rousseau draws attention is the difficulty of retaining the state of mind of tranquility in the world outside the island. And this I notice is an anxiety of mine—one, too, of the other retreatants—as I return to my quotidian life after the retreat. How can I keep hold of some of the sense of being centered, more at one with myself, less distracted, when I have to get on with my work and when I am confronted by others, some of whom, unlike my fellow retreatants, are difficult and awkward to deal with? And it might seem that the issue here is that I have the sense—and Rousseau had the sense—that, really, life ought to be like this all the time, that is, as it is during the retreat. Could we not arrange things such that it would be? But in fact, the problem is much deeper and more subtle than that. For what one knows—and this is the second point about the light cast on the world for Rousseau by his stay on the island—what one knows is not simply that life cannot ever be like this in its totality, that it is not given to human beings to live in this way, but that it would not be good to live this way even if it were possible. Rousseau is quite explicit on this point, though, I think, he passes over it rather too quickly. For, discussing the wonderful state of mind he experienced and whether others too have experienced it, he says that he thinks they have not, or, at least, have done so so "imperfectly" that they really do not know how lovely it is. And then he says: "It would not even be good . . . if, hungry for this gentle rapture, they lost their taste for an active life in which their needs, forever being renewed, prescribe for them their work [devoir]."[6] Rousseau's point here is that the work of the world can be done only if we do not give ourselves up to the kinds of delight he found on La Motte. The point here is not that peace of mind, tranquility, happens not to be found in the work of the world, as if this were a mere contingency. It is, rather, that the absence of such tranquility—expressed in ambition, longing, competition, rivalry, and so on—is crucial for there being such a world at all. There is no human world without these things. Or, to put the point another way, there can be no utopia for human beings; there is no condition in which they can be at peace with themselves, that is, no such condition as a permanent state of their living together. Conflict, rivalry, and the like are essential to what it is to be a human being. The most that one can have are the occasional moments, short periods of tranquility of the kind that Rousseau found on St. Peter's Island. Or, if someone or some group of people were to seek to live always in such a state—as in communities of monks, say—they can do this only on the assumption that the overwhelming majority of the others do not do so. For sure, this is not to deny that one can do something to bring some measure of tranquility to everyday life, a carryover, as it were, from a period of meditation. One might even, perhaps, find one's whole life shot through with a deeper sense of peace, a more developed or sensitive skillfulness, as the Buddhists like to say. But even so, the restlessness of the world is bound to impose itself on one sooner or later, and then the issue is one of managing it all in a better way; and to claim that this could always involve peace of mind is surely little more than a desperate hope.

Yet, as Rousseau so marvelously brings out, his state of being on La Motte gives him this sense: *this* is where one finds the meaning of life; *here* is how one should live, could live. This means, I think, that he has the sense that he has seen what the meaning of life is, but that it cannot be lived out. And there is something profound in this that resonates with us all, I think: the idea that the meaning of one's life, of life, is just there, just over the horizon of one's quotidian concerns, but that it is always elusive, can be glimpsed but not fully absorbed into one's life.

Virginia Woolf said that she wrote her novel *The Waves*, not to a plot, but to a rhythm. Woolf intended that rhythm to alert us to a relation to the world that is at once an imaginative investment in it and also a revelation of what is there to be seen if only we can open our eyes. This is partly a matter of the content of the novel: the characters themselves live in and through their imagination, and this investment saturates their lives so that one does not know where their "real" life ends and their dream life begins. Or rather, it puts that very distinction in question. By what measure do we decide that someone's imaginative life is not part of his or her "real" life? We operate all the time with simplistic conceptions of identity, as if we could definitively say what does and what does not belong to the narrative, to the fabric, of someone's life. But decisions as to such matters are always to a greater or lesser extent arbitrary, even if there are some things that clearly do not belong to such a narrative. Or we might say: each of us leads many lives at the same time, and they overlap in complex ways, sometimes mutually antagonistically, sometimes nourishing each other. Here is an example of the kind of imaginative investment in things that the characters in Woolf's novel make. It is from very early in the work, when they are all still in prep school:

> "Now they have all gone," said Louis. "I am alone. They have gone into the house for breakfast, and I am left standing by the wall among the flowers. It is very early, before lessons. Flower after flower is specked on the depths of green. The petals are harlequins. Stalks rise from the black hollows beneath. The flowers swim like fish made of light upon the dark, green waters. I hold a stalk in my hand. I am the stalk. My roots go down to the depths of the world, through earth dry with brick, and damp earth, through veins of lead and silver. I am all fibre. All tremors shake me, and the weight of the earth is pressed to my ribs. Up here my eyes are green leaves, unseeing. I am a boy in grey flannels with a belt fastened by a brass snake up here. Down there my eyes are the lidless eyes of a stone figure in a desert by the Nile. I see women passing with red pitchers to the river; I see camels swaying and men in turbans. I hear tramplings, tremblings, stirrings round me."[7]

But the issue is not simply that of entering into Louis's imaginative world, though it is that. It is that the writing itself has an immensely sensuous, tactile, material quality to it, as if the words were material and lifted themselves off the page to touch us, like a breeze playing through our hair as we read, or sunlight caressing our skin. And part of this is Woolf's repeated insistence that the mind is material: words in the mind are material, and this is both cause and effect of the materiality of the mind itself. Bernard is being washed by a housemistress at the prep school:

> "Mrs Constable, girt in a bath-towel, takes her lemon-coloured sponge and soaks it in water; it turns chocolate-brown; it drips; and, holding it high above me, shivering beneath her, she squeezes it. Water pours down the runnel of my spine. Bright arrows of sensation shoot on either side. I am covered with warm flesh. My dry crannies are wetted; my cold body is warmed; it is sluiced and gleaming. Water descends and sheets me like an eel. Now hot towels envelop me, and their roughness, as I rub my back, makes my blood purr. Rich and heavy sensations form on the roof of my mind; down showers the day. . . . Pouring down the walls of my mind, running together, the day falls copious, resplendent."[8]

The mind has a roof and walls, and water flows through it as it flows across his body; the water's flowing down his body *is* the water's flowing through his mind. Woolf's sense of the mind as material has nothing to do with what is called materialism in the philosophy of mind. Rather, she means that there is simply no way in which the mind can be understood without thinking of it in the same kind of material terms that we use to understand the world around us. Neville, says Bernard to himself, has "a mind like the tongue of an ant-eater, rapid, dexterous, glutinous."[9] Woolf says to us: any translation of that thought into something that we might deem "literal," anything that avoids this simile in the name of greater truth or accuracy, will end up with less of both. Were we to excise this way of thinking of the mind from our understanding, we should simply be handicapping ourselves, truncating our capacity to understand ourselves and each other. *The Waves* says this to us: the thinking we need to understand the mind is seamlessly continuous with that which we need to understand the body and the material world more generally. The vocabulary of the mind is of a piece with that of the body. Or we might say: the body thinks and the mind is just part of the body.

In a marvelous essay on Woolf, W. H. Auden said this of her, quoting her to help make his point:

> What she felt and expressed with the most intense passion was a mystical, religious vision of life, "a consciousness of what I call 'reality': a thing I see before me: something abstract; but residing in the downs or sky; beside which nothing matters; in which I shall exist and continue to exist. . . . How difficult not to go making 'reality' this and that, whereas it is one thing. Now perhaps this is my gift: this perhaps is what distinguishes me from other people: I think it may be rare to have so acute a sense of something like that—but again, who knows? I would like to express it too."
>
> What is unique about her work is the combination of this mystical vision with the sharpest possible sense for the concrete, even in its humblest form: "One can't," she observes, "write directly about the soul. Looked at, it vanishes; but look at the ceiling, at Grizzle, at the cheaper beasts in the Zoo which are exposed to walkers in Regent's Park, and the soul slips in."[10]

Woolf's point about writing about the ceiling, which lets the soul slip in, is another way, among other things, I

91

think, of expressing what I have already said about the material nature of the mind.

So the sensuous quality of Woolf's writing is its responsiveness to, its expression of, a religious or mystical sense of life. For Woolf, everything that *is* bespeaks something else, something that cannot be said, something behind or beside it, the thing it really is, but which escapes expression. The particular rhythm of *The Waves* everywhere expresses the sense of the material world as saturated with the mystical, the material world *as* mystical, which is why, for Woolf, that world touches us, makes us *feel* things, so intensely.

Woolf invites us to slow down, to stop, as Rousseau slowed down and stopped, aware, of course, that the exigencies of life constantly pull us away from the vision of the world that she explores, constantly *conceal* the world from us. We need to be jolted, woken up by something that makes us realize the truth of Woolf's vision. In a sense, I think that all Woolf's writing aims to jolt us in this way, and, when we are woken, at least for a moment we experience a deeply rapturous sense of the material world. So Alphonso Lingis writes:

> While reading on the porch, to wake up to a hummingbird sizzling in the sheets of sunlight. To wake up to the grain of the old wood of the porch railing, enigmatic as a fossil of some long-extinct reptile. . . . Awakening is proud and hopeful. The interruption of continuity makes possible the leap, with all the forces of the present, into what is ahead. It makes possible hope, the awaiting what cannot reasonably be expected.[11]

When I think of the writers who mean most to me, I find that I seek in some of them this awakening—Rilke, for example, or D. H. Lawrence. I go to them so that they poke me in the ribs and wake me up. In a different way, it is also there in Orwell, who loved so much what he called the "surface of the earth and the process of life—which . . . is *not* the same thing as wanting to have a good time and stay alive as long as possible."[12] I hardly know a better expression of this love of the surface of the world than something John Berger said:

> What reconciles me to my own death more than anything else is the image of a place: a place where your bones and mine are buried, thrown, uncovered, together. They are strewn there pell-mell. One of your ribs leans against my skull. A metacarpal of my left hand lies inside your pelvis. (Against my broken ribs your breast like a flower.) The hundred bones of our feet are scattered like gravel. It is strange that this image of our proximity, concerning as it does mere phosphate of calcium, should bestow a sense of peace. Yet it does. With you I can imagine a place where to be phosphate of calcium is enough.[13]

▶ ▷ ▶

When I go on the weeklong retreat, as I mentioned, one of the things I do is to work in the garden: the center grows much of its own food, and the retreatants help with this work, planting seeds or planting out seedlings, hoeing and weeding, watering, and so on. I am very lucky to have a

93

small garden at my home in London too, where I grow jasmine and roses and salvia and lavender, among other things. Gardening can, of course, be done as everything can be done, namely, impatiently and inattentively. But there would be little point in that. In his book *A Philosophy of Gardens*, David E. Cooper suggests that "many garden practices *induce* virtues," and he makes clear that what he means by "induce" is "attract," "invite," "bring on," "entail"— and that, for this to be the case, "those practices . . . [have to be] engaged in with a proper understanding and appreciation of what they are." "Certain garden-practices necessarily induce virtues," he writes. Using the example of a man who grows a squash in his garden, Cooper says of him that he must know how to care for the plant as it grows and that this discipline of caring for the plant "and his garden as a whole imposes a structure and pattern on a life that might otherwise be lacking in shape and unity. . . . [This] virtue of care for life in the garden modulates, one might say, into care of self." Further, the mature squash is a kind of "gift," a matter of "grace," and this induces the virtue of humility, a virtue connected, says Cooper, with hope, the virtue of placing trust or faith in the "co-operation of the world" with one's efforts and endeavor. This hope is not mere wishful thinking but, he says, drawing on some comments made by John Cottingham, an "'emotional allegiance' to 'the power of goodness' in one's intercourse with nature and other human beings," and he thinks of this as "a 'foundational' virtue—a pre-condition for the exercise of any others."[14]

Now, I am sure it is true that gardening *could* have such rewards in terms of virtue, virtue, that is, not simply as one goes about the gardening, but for one's life overall, and perhaps it does in some cases. But it is striking that the claims Cooper makes here for gardening are parallel to those made by many other philosophers for an engagement with literature—novels and the like—in moral education. It is no doubt true that being a sensitive reader of novels *could* sharpen one's imaginative insight into the plight of others and so develop one's care or compassion for them, or that it *could* help one develop fortitude or temperance or courage or whatever by seeing how fictional characters negotiate the vicissitudes of their life. But, unfortunately, there is no doubt whatever that it is possible to be a fine reader of literature and be thoroughly selfish when it comes to others. Indeed, one's attention to literature might be bought at the price of inattention to others. Furthermore, I might well be able sensitively to appreciate a fictional person's courage while remaining utterly craven in my own life. Similarly, the whole of Cooper's argument begs the question by insisting that certain garden practices necessarily induce the virtues in those who go about them "with a proper understanding and appreciation of what they are"—for he will always be able to claim that anyone who goes in for gardening and in whom the virtues are not cultivated, both within and without the garden, is not going about it the right way with the right understanding. But there can be selfish and mean people who are nonetheless wonderful gardeners.

Cooper's argument, as that of those who reason in similar ways when thinking about our engagement with literature, is an extended exercise in trying to straighten out the world. Although it is presented as exploring how the world actually is, really it is an exercise in describing how Cooper would like the world to be. I too would like the world to be this way, but things are more shambolic than Cooper would like to admit, and the human soul is less of a piece than he imagines. It may be painful to behold, but someone who is gentle and tender with his or her plants might be cold and indifferent with the human beings around him or her. It is *much easier* to be kind to plants than to people. And someone might, in his garden, allow its rhythms to impose a certain pattern on his activities while remaining utterly inept at caring for his own self: his life might be chaotic, shambolic, self-destructive everywhere but in his garden—which is why he might like being there so much. Indeed, Rousseau's life was.

We should not, I think, moralize the rapture that can come from being in a garden and from working there. When I work in the garden on retreat, or when I cultivate the flowers in my garden at home, I often lose myself in the work and experience delight in the contact with the soil, in the scent of the flowers, in watching seeds germinate and grow, in planting a seedling and nursing it as it grows and so on. If any of this makes me a morally or ethically better person, it is only because it makes me happy, and when I am happy it is easier for me to be kind to others and to myself. Indeed, those philosophers who claim, following a line of thought that goes back at least to Plato, that if you are virtuous you will be happy never seem to want to explore the converse thought, which, in my view, has much more to be said for it: that if you are happy you are more likely to be virtuous. That may, in the end, be no more plausible than the converse thought. I just do not know. But, at any rate, the rapture of gardening is sufficient unto itself.

5
The Kiss
Creation and Love

And while he yet spake, lo, Judas, one of the twelve, came, and with him a great multitude with swords and staves, from the chief priests and elders of the people.

Now he that betrayed him gave them a sign, saying, Whomsoever I shall kiss, that same is he: hold him fast.

And forthwith he came to Jesus, and said, Hail, master; and kissed him.

And Jesus said unto him, Friend, wherefore art thou come? Then came they, and laid hands on Jesus and took him.

(Matthew 26:47–50)

No Judas, no crucifixion; no crucifixion, no resurrection; no resurrection, no Christianity. And no Christianity, no Western culture as we know it, that very particular form in which the usual ways of humanity—barbarity, squalor, cruelty, greed, and idiocy; splendor, wisdom, love, beauty, and generosity—have shaped the West. A kiss is one of those things foundational for Western culture as a whole, that utterly breathtaking combination of megalomaniacal destruction and magnificent creation.

Why is there no philosophy of the kiss, one of the most rapturous experiences of which human beings are capable? As it so often does, philosophy rushes on too quickly, keen to get to that which it deems more important (from where does it get its measure of importance?), overlooking that which it takes to be too—what? local? minor?—for philosophical study. But imagine what human life would be like without kisses. Think of all the longing, joy, tenderness, despair, revulsion—all of that between parents and children; friends; lovers; enemies—of which human life would be stripped without kissing. Who could think this unworthy of philosophical attention? Philosophy should be ashamed of its inattention. But it is proud of it, mistaking it for a way of dealing with more important matters (this is part, one might say, of philosophy's self-congratulatory temptation, which betrays its better possibilities).

A kiss can be foundational for a life, too. The young Marcel's plot to experience his mother's goodnight kiss in Proust's *À la recherche du temps perdu* finds its place at the outset of, expresses and informs, his whole madly self-destructive, glorious life. Simone Weil's revulsion as a little girl when a friend of the family, visiting them in their Paris apartment, kissed her on the hand sounded the keynote of her life: she ran screaming from the room to wash off the gentleman's saliva, just as she sought later to rid herself of all that bound her to the earth.

But the secret of the rapture of a kiss is perhaps best known by Chekhov in his story "The Kiss." The protagonist is Staff-Captain Ryabovich, a lonely, unconfident, timid, awkward, and unloved officer. His artillery brigade is billeted, late in May, in the village of Mestechki, and the officers receive an invitation from the local squire, Lieutenant-General von Rabbeck, to come to tea. All nineteen of them make their way to the squire's house, though the thought of going there rather bores them all: they are tired and just want some quiet for the evening. Von Rabbeck himself is not so enthusiastic: he has invited them because it is good form to do so, the done thing. And, in any case, it is not convenient as he has guests staying already: two sisters and their children have turned up, along with his brothers and some neighbors.

After tea, the officers go into the ballroom. Many of them dance—but not Ryabovich, who has never danced in his life, never put his arm round a woman's waist. He is sad, but this is, it seems to him, his lot in life.

A couple of the officers, at von Rabbeck's invitation, head off to play billiards, and Ryabovich trudges off after them. He watches the game for a while and then wanders off, bored. But he gets lost in the maze of rooms, and, fumbling from one room to the next, he finds himself in a small, completely dark room. Then, suddenly, a woman rushes up to him, cries out "At last!" and puts her arms round his neck, kissing him softly as she places her burning cheek on his. She is clearly waiting for her lover and, in the darkness, has mistaken Ryabovich for the man for whom she is waiting. She recoils and flees, Ryabovich meanwhile rushing toward the chink of light in the door through which he has come.

The effect on him is profound. He

gave himself up to a totally new kind of sensation, one he had never experienced before in all his life. Something strange was happening to him . . . his neck, which just a few minutes ago had been embraced by sweet-smelling hands, seemed anointed with oil. And on his left cheek, just by his moustache, there was a faint, pleasant, cold, tingling sensation, the kind you get from peppermint drops, and the more he rubbed the spot the stronger the tingling became.[1]

Suddenly, Ryabovich's whole state is changed. He is in a state of joy and lightness of spirit that is utterly new to him. He feels that he has entered into a new life, a life where things are radiant and the people in the squire's house are endlessly interested and pleasing.

Ryabovich is well aware, of course, that the kiss was intended for another, but he nonetheless remains in a state of rapture and, looking at all the women present, tries to fathom who it was who kissed him in the dark room. It is all to no avail, of course. Nonetheless, he spends the summer thinking of the mysterious woman and the kiss she gave him until, at the end of August, he finds himself once again in the vicinity of von Rabbeck's house. It is here that he realizes the complete absurdity of his longing, of the pointlessness of his self-deception over the summer, as if he might have been loved by the woman who kissed him: he goes to the house and no one is there; all is dark; and the towels in von Rabbeck's bathing hut by the river are cold and rough. Ryabovich is overwhelmed by a feeling of stupidity and futility—his own and the world's. All suddenly strikes him as meaningless. When he returns to his camp he is told by his batman that all the officers have gone to "General Fontryabkin's." Ryabovich lies down on his bed and does not go to the general's.

Chekhov reminds us of the power of a kiss. In some ways, it is the most intimate physical gesture that can bind two people together. This is particularly so with respect to kisses on another's mouth. Traditionally, prostitutes do not kiss. When one thinks about it, this is incredible, given what they do do—than which, one might suppose, there could be nothing more intimate. It is as if kissing were *more* intimate than sex. But then why are there no prostitutes whose service to clients is that of kissing on the mouth and nothing else? It is as if the one thing that someone might *really* want in going to a prostitute were the most intimate physical contact with him or her possible. But that is to kiss and be kissed on the mouth. Somehow this gets misidentified as if what one really wanted was sex. Kissing is both much less than sex—this is obvious—but also, less obviously, much more. It is that *more* that the prostitute will not give, as if it might entangle him or her—and the client, therefore—in a kind of intimacy that is utterly compromising and cannot be paid off with money; that is, in a real intimacy that having sex in the context of a financial contract cannot provide.

It is peculiar that in French *baiser* means both "to fuck" and "to kiss." The noun is *le baiser*. But the French tend to use *(la) bise* and *(des) bisous* where in English we would use "kiss(es)" or may just say (as at the end of a letter) "love" or "lots of love." *Embrasser* means "to embrace" but is usually used in the meaning of "to kiss" and is the usual term used in everyday French—for example, at the end of a telephone call *(Je t'embrasse)*. In all the delicate negotiations, therefore, that the French language makes with these terms, we

might say we see a sense of the way in which kissing both
is and is not a sexual gesture, both, as I said, more intimate than sex and less so; or, as it were, the apotheosis of
sex, its most perfect expression, what sex really is, and yet
less than that because it is, of course, after all, only kissing.
Perhaps it is on account of the delicate relations that kissing has with sex that, as Adam Phillips has noted, kissing,
unlike other sexual activity, has developed no familiar
slang, for it both is and is not a sexual activity. At least this
is so in English. The French have more slang for kissing
on the mouth, and it is, perhaps, telling that we speak in
English of French kissing (not to mention the now dated
term for a condom: French letter).

So why should kissing another on the mouth be more
intimate that sex? It must, surely, have to do with the way it
evokes an intimacy with another's *face*, the place where we
see another in all his or her individuality. Your face is *where
you are*. Your body has a kind of impersonality that your
face never has.

To see this, I offer this thought. A while ago I took part
in a public debate during a philosophy festival on the topic
of love and sex. One of the interlocutors in the debate was
a woman who had worked as a high-class call girl in London in order to finance her PhD degree. During the discussion she said something in particular that I found to be
of extreme interest. She said that, when she would first
meet the man who had paid for her services and with
whom she was to spend the next hour or evening or whatever, she would have to find something of interest in him
where otherwise she might have been utterly indifferent.
Otherwise, she said, the time spent with him would have
been unbearable for her. She clearly intended this as a way

of ascribing a certain generosity to the work of a call girl, a way of casting it in a light that one might, I suppose, not readily have imagined. But for me the key point is this: when you want to make love with a person, when you want to kiss a person, this is because he or she is *already* interesting to you: you do not need to find something of interest; you are already interested. But in the case of a call girl—or rent boy or whatever—the interest has to be *found*, in a way conjured out of nothing, because the focus here is the body, and the body is impersonal. If I want to kiss your mouth, I want to kiss *you*; if the call girl is willing to have sex with this man, she is willing to have sex with him, not as the specific man he is, but as any man, as a representative of men as such with no specific individuality. And even if the client knows this, as he surely does, the call girl's attempt to find something interesting in him can, so to speak, save the situation for him too by allowing him to indulge the fantasy—which of course he knows to be false—that she wants to be with *him*, not just *some* man, whoever he may be. The call girl's finding something interesting in the client to whom she would otherwise be utterly indifferent—or, perhaps, by whom she might be revolted— allows them both to engage in a mutually sustaining fantasy that allows the transaction—the sex for money—to take place.

This brings us back to Chekhov's story with an ability to appreciate a moment of great profundity. Ryabovich, I noted, after he has had his encounter and when he is back in the hall with the other guests, looks at all the women present and tries to imagine which of them had mistakenly kissed him. He tells himself that she must be young, since older ladies do not have such rendezvous; and, he supposes, intelligent: "I could tell from the rustle of her dress, her smell, her voice." It is, of course, quite impossible to judge a person's intelligence from such matters, and there is a typical piece of Chekhovian comedy here, but the key point here is that Ryabovich desperately wants to fix on the individuality of the woman who kissed him so that he can imagine—that is, entertain in fantasy, despite his knowing it not to be the case—that it was *he* whom she wanted to kiss. For if he knows who she is—which of the women present—then he can imagine her desires as the desires of *this* woman. And if he can imagine (fantasize) that, he can imagine that she wanted to kiss *him*. The kiss would remain otherwise merely an utterly impersonal gesture in which the woman in question would be no more interested in him than a call girl is in her client.

But Ryabovich finds the fantasy hard to sustain: there is so little to go on. And it is here that we see Chekhov's depth of insight. Ryabovich is caught between the desire (fantasy) that *this* woman be the woman who kissed him and the terrible impersonality of the gesture. So he keeps imagining that the woman was *this* woman whom he sees in the hall of the house, but he also cannot avoid the collapse of that desire and finding that the woman who gave him the kiss was, after all, rather *like* this specific woman, not actually this woman at all.

> He stared at the girl in lilac and found her very attractive. She had beautiful shoulders and arms, a clever face and a fine voice. As he gazed at her, Ryabovich wanted *her*, no one else, to be that mysterious stranger. . . . But she gave a rather artificial laugh and wrinkled her long nose, which made her look old. Then he turned to the blonde in black.

She was younger, simpler and less affected, with charming temples and she sipped daintily from her wine glass. Now Ryabovich wanted her to be the stranger. But he soon discovered that she has a featureless face and he turned to her neighbour. . . ."It's hard to say," he wondered dreamily. "If I could just take the lilac girl's shoulders and arms away, add the blonde's temples, then take those eyes away from the girl on Lobytko's left, *then.*" He merged them all into one, so that he had an image of the girl who had kissed him, the image he desired so much, but which he could not find among the guests around the table.[2]

Ryabovich wants *this specific girl* to be the one, but it always turns out that *a girl rather like this* is the girl who kissed him. He knows that the kiss was wholly impersonal: given by an unknown woman to the wrong man. But he desperately wants it to be personal. There is no more of the personal in the whole event than in the call girl's meeting of the client. He knows this and seeks to fantasize it away, as the call girl and her client engage in a mutually sustaining fantasy to fantasize away the utter impersonality of the transaction between them. Ryabovich is, so to speak, in the position of the call girl's client, but seeking to do all the work of fantasy alone, though I do not mean of course that this is how he represents things to himself. That would be to overintellectualize the issue. I am, rather, offering an analysis of the meaning of what is going on in him as his eye and mind glide from one woman to another among those present.

You are where your face is, I said; you are in your face. If I want to kiss your mouth, I want to kiss you, the specific person you are, and this, I have suggested, is why kissing in this way is more intimate than sex. But if I want to kiss you on the mouth, there is still more to be said to understand the peculiar intimacy of this.

John Keats famously referred to lips as "slippery blisses." I should perhaps say "infamously" because many have been at least faintly revolted by the phrase. But surely part of the revulsion is that kissing another on the mouth, on the lips, always places itself in the vicinity of disgust: I might find it disgusting that you can want to kiss *that* mouth (which I find repellent); and, even as I wish to kiss *this* mouth, I am well aware that part of the intense pleasure is that someone else's tongue in my mouth can be experienced as utterly disgusting. The peculiar intimacy, delight, of my having your tongue in my mouth, and your having mine in yours, depends in part in the recognition that such a thing—having someone else's tongue in one's mouth—can be a disgusting affront. "Slippery blisses" are lips, but they are kisses too. When Raymond, played by Dustin Hoffman in the film *Rain Man* (1988), is kissed by his brother's girlfriend, she asks him what the experience was for him. "Wet," he replies. The wetness of kissing hovers always close to disgust. I might be overwhelmingly excited by kissing you and feeling the wetness of your saliva in my mouth; but your saliva spat out into a glass will disgust me intensely, especially so should you invite me to take it into my mouth. Raymond's comment strips kissing of all that is rapturous—*and* reminds us why kissing is apt to be so delicious.

I am, then, following Keats on kisses in seeking to explain their peculiar intimacy, greater than that of sex. Christopher Ricks puts it marvelously:

Keats intimates that a full kiss upon the lips is uniquely moving and creative, and that it is so because of its dewiness and because of its reciprocity, the rhyme of lips upon lips. And perhaps because of the impossibility of talking at that moment, the relief from talk, since this poesy, this rhyme, is not a matter of saying anything. Moreover, you cannot kiss your own mouth . . . and this for a more total reason than that you cannot kiss some parts of yourself; the full sense of self in a kiss upon the lips is supremely dependent upon non-self and its perfect complement. For Keats, a kiss is creative, an act of love which makes love; as is well known, we kiss not only because we love but so that we may love.[3]

It is *this* that Chekhov knows, and it is this that Ryabovich knows. And the latter spends a summer in a state of fantasy because he wanted so deeply to possess this rapture for himself. His final realization that it is not to be his shatters him and his sense of the meaning of things because this form of creative love has escaped him when it seemed so close.

▶ ▷ ▶

Émile Zola's *Thérèse Raquin* is, as has been pointed out many times, a fairly lurid novel, but I am not sure that it has often been noted how it draws our attention to the kiss as a gesture of magic. Thérèse and Laurent, her lover, have murdered the former's husband, Camille, that they may be together. Laurent drowned him when the three were out boating for the afternoon. But as Laurent pitched Camille over into the water, Camille managed to bite him hard on the neck, and the scar then acts as a perpetual reminder to Laurent of his deed: it continues to ache and sting, a physical aspect of his moral suffering as he seeks to escape from his increasing remorse at his deed.

Camille's body remained in the water for two weeks, and Laurent went each day to the Paris mortuary to see if the corpse had finally been found: at that time, unidentified bodies—mainly those of children—were laid out for viewing in the mortuary through a large window, the corpses being kept under running water to delay the process of decay. After several visits, he finally sees the man he has murdered. He is horrified by the appearance of the body: decayed flesh, discolored to a monstrous green, battered, the sides split open, the ribs breaking through. He does not speak of this to Thérèse, but later, when they are married, she asks him about it. His reply is at once evasive and telling.

"Kiss me," he said to her, offering her his neck.

Thérèse had got up, completely pale in her nightclothes; she leant back a little, her elbow resting on the marble of the mantlepiece. She looked at Laurent's neck. She had just noticed, on the whiteness of his skin, a pink mark. A rush of blood to Laurent's head made the mark larger and it took on a fiery red colour.

"Kiss me, kiss me," repeated Laurent, his face and neck burning.

The young woman bent her head further back to avoid the kiss and, placing the tip of her finger on Camille's bite, asked her husband:

"What's that? I didn't know you had a wound there."

THE KISS

It seemed to Laurent that Thérèse's finger was boring a
hole in his neck. Feeling the touch of her finger he started
back, uttering a soft cry of pain.

"That," he stammered, "that . . ."

He hesitated, but he could not lie and told her the truth
in spite of himself.

"Camille bit me, you know, in the boat. It's nothing, it's
healed . . . Kiss me, kiss me."

And the wretched man held out his burning neck. He
wanted Thérèse to kiss him on the scar, counting on the
kiss of this woman to calm the thousand stings that were
tearing at his flesh. His chin raised, holding out his neck,
he offered himself. Thérèse, more or less lying on the
mantlepiece, made a gesture of deep disgust and cried out
in a pleading voice:

"Oh, no, not there . . .! There's blood on it."

She fell back into a low chair, trembling, her head in her
hands. Laurent was stunned. He lowered his chin and looked
at Thérèse distractedly. Then, suddenly, as if his grip were
that of a wild animal, he took her head in his large hands
and forced her lips onto his neck, on Camille's bite. For a
moment he kept the head of this woman crushed against
his skin. Thérèse did not struggle, just gave dull cries, sti-
fled against Laurent's neck. When she got away from him
she wiped her mouth savagely and spat into the fireplace.
She had not said a word.[4]

In no literal sense, of course, could Thérèse's kiss heal
Laurent's scar. But the kiss Laurent so deeply needs is rich
with meaning. To receive it would be a gesture to seal their
complicity: Laurent and Thérèse had planned the murder
together, but it was he who committed the deed in the

most literal physical sense, while Thérèse looked on from one end of the boat, and the *physical* gesture of the kiss would thus symbolize for him what one might call a complicity of the physical deed and so offer him succor. Beyond that, the kiss would express her total love and acceptance of him and offer the kind of comfort that we offer when our child scrapes his or her knee and we offer to "kiss it better." The kiss would heal not literally—the scar would remain—but magically: the scar's meaning would be altered, and it is just this that Laurent cannot have from Thérèse. And he cannot have it because she is as guilty as he, so cannot heal—absolve him—in this way. He wants a *magical* complicity in guilt that would provide relief for him—a shared guilt in sin. But she is desperate for her guilt with him not to be sealed by that gesture, which allows her to retain some—deceptive, but nonetheless, for her, significant—sense of her own freedom from a total, all-annihilating guilt.

But all this depends on the *magical* quality of the kiss more generally, for without the sense of this Laurent could not desire Thérèse's kiss as he does. A kiss is magical because, as Keats intimates, it is creative. If I kiss a picture of my lover it is not because I think that this will effect any change in her: there is no causal chain set in motion from my kiss of her photograph to her well-being, and no such kiss can offer concrete, worldly protection to her. Nor is it, exactly, that this kiss expresses my love or desire for her; though it does that, that is not the central issue, I think. Rather, what is at stake here is that the kiss simply in and of itself seems *fitting*. And there is much like that in human life: gestures, words that are fitting and appropriate, but our explanation of why this is so is limited and peters out, and we can say nothing more—and nothing less—than, as Wittgenstein would say, "This is what we do." A kiss is creative because it carries a whole strand of our culture with it: its possible meanings of love, desire, forgiveness, reverence, affection, ritual, amity, and so on are there when we kiss. When I kiss another a whole culture speaks through my lips, whether I know it or not, including all that I have seen and known of kissing from observing others, from novels, from plays, from films, and from much else besides. In many of our gestures and deeds, in our words and exclamations, we express a massive surfeit of complex cultural meanings: we are never alone in these things and our cultural world—ethical, religious, political—is speaking through us in them. A kiss is a piece of magic because it is a peculiarly intense, compacted, rich gesture in this way.

111

(I remark in passing that Thérèse's spitting into the fireplace trades on the cultural freight of spitting. To spit in someone's face is an attack that goes well beyond the physical harm it might cause. There is, for example, a peculiar horror and degradation in the punishment Jean-Baptiste Clamence speaks of in Camus's *La Chute* in which the prisoner is immobilized, standing upright, such that each warder can spit copiously on his face. And we should note that Marcel in Proust's *À la recherche du temps perdu* forms his very notion of sadism from overhearing Mlle Vinteuil and her friend speaking of spitting on the photograph of the former's father. Marcel has no doubt that this is an evil deed, which it is, and it helps us deepen our sense both of the meaning of a person's photograph and of the fact that we may in the end not be able to make much sense of the notion of evil without the concept of desecration, hence without a religious context.)

Why is it that a kiss, of all things, is so massively freighted with such cultural meanings? No doubt it is in part because of what Phillips calls the mouth's "extraordinary virtuosity," its role particularly in both eating and speech, the former linking us so powerfully with the other animals, the latter marking us off from them, but we shall certainly arrive pretty quickly at the thought there is a mystery here: this is just one of those things that make us the kind of creatures we are. As I noted earlier, human life would be unrecognizable without kisses.

Laurent is in a state of agony. He thought he could kill Camille and get Thérèse, but what he got was himself as a murderer, and that displaced Thérèse entirely from his life. Laurent, we might say, loses his humanity in his remorse but, in doing so, is all the more brought up face to face with it in himself. For it is one of the marks of our human life that we can lose our humanity; no animal can lose its animality. We can lose what we are and in this way be all the more submerged in it. Samuel Johnson remarked that he who makes a beast of himself forgets the pain of being a man. He might have added: but he also feels it even more keenly.

► ▷ ►

Until a few years ago I had seen only reproductions of Rembrandt's *The Jewish Bride*. I nodded in agreement as I read in many critics that this painting was a supreme manifestation of marital love: it was obvious even from the reproductions that the work was a masterpiece. But then I found myself in Amsterdam and saw the painting in the Rijksmuseum. I was stunned. No reproduction of the work can even begin to convey the profound tenderness that the painting expresses and offers to the viewer. The center of the painting is to be found, of course, in the touching hands. These hands are kissing. The faces of the man and woman are irradiated with love for each other, a delicacy, a tenderness, a gentleness beyond compare. But they are not even looking at each other. Their faces are not touching. Yet their lips are touching: there is a diagonal from the top left toward the bottom right of the canvas that follows the lines of their lips and is parallel to the line, moving in the same way but lower down, through the man's sleeve, along his arm, into his right hand, and then on to her left hand. We are invited to see the lips touching as the hands are touching. More exactly, their kiss is held in abeyance and yet intimated in the placing of the hands. These hands are among the most marvelous ever painted in Western art, and they are so, in part, because they have the personality of the lips. It is not incidental to Rembrandt's purposes that, after the face, the hands are the most individuating features of the human body: your hands tell me who you are, what you have done with your life; they carry the traces of your work, your deeds.

The experience one has in looking at this painting is that one has never before seen—really *seen*—a human body, grasped what a human body is, what it is to have, to be, a human body. Schopenhauer said that, in the experience of art, the struggling, suffering will is stilled, and here, finally, one comes to rest. In front of Rembrandt's *The Jewish Bride*, the will is stilled in a rapture of amazement that anyone can see so deeply and clearly what we as human beings are—and what a kiss can mean to us.

6

Nothingness

The Disappearance of a Man and a Woman

On Friday, June 12, 2009, a man boarded a bus in Derry and traveled to Sligo on the Irish coast. Once there, he checked into a hotel for three nights—a weekend from Friday to Monday. He gave his name at the reception as Peter Bergmann, together with an address in Vienna, paying in advance for his room in cash. Over the course of the weekend, he was seen going in and out of the hotel on many occasions, each time carrying a purple plastic bag, clearly with things in it, and each time returning without anyone being able to see the bag; presumably, it was in his pocket. Many of the staff saw his movements in and out of the hotel; his comings and goings were also caught on the hotel security cameras.

He was disposing of whatever it was that was in the carrier bag. Sligo has numerous CCTV cameras, but not one of them captured images of where he was disposing of the material. Moreover, an extensive search carried out later of the bins in Sligo turned up nothing connected with him.

Gardens, public spaces, car parks, and the local dump were also searched, and nothing was found.

On the Sunday morning he took a taxi to the beach at Rosses Point near Sligo. Once there, he got out of the taxi, looked at the beach, got back into the taxi and returned to Sligo.

Bergmann left the hotel at 1 p.m. on the Monday, walking to the bus station. Along the way, he disposed of a black holdall bag—never recovered—with which he had left the hotel. At the bus station he had with him the purple bag, along with a bag slung over his shoulder, of the type used to carry a laptop. From the bus station he took a bus to Rosses Point. A number of people saw him walking on the beach that afternoon and into the evening, when the sun had almost completely set and it was already rather dark.

Bergmann's body was found around 6.30 a.m. on the Tuesday morning by a local man who was walking on the beach. He was with his son, and the two of them said the Lord's Prayer over the body.

Bergmann had removed all the labels in the clothing he was wearing, making it impossible to trace where he had bought it. Despite the fact that his body was found on the beach, there was no external evidence of saltwater drowning. The autopsy showed that he had previously been subject to heart attacks and that he had been suffering from cancer of the prostate, with tumor found also in the bone. There was no evidence of his having taken any analgesics to cope with the pain that such an extensive cancer must have been causing him.

Peter Bergmann never existed, and the address he gave in Vienna was fake. Despite extensive research both nationally and internationally, using fingerprint and DNA evidence, no trace of a Peter Bergmann answering this man's description has to date been found.

People disappear all the time, often in unexplained circumstances. But it is clear that this man wanted much more than to disappear. He wanted completely to erase his identity. He wanted never to have existed. He wanted to be, to have been, nothing.

► ▷ ►

How are we to understand this troubling and fascinating case? What is at stake philosophically in this man's erasure of his identity? What does it mean to want to erase any evidence that one has ever existed, to be nothing?

Peter Bergmann's project bears an uncanny resemblance to Simone Weil's project in her later philosophy. Central to her thinking is the concept of the void (*le vide*). At one level, she thinks that this is what each of us actually is: a void. But we seek all the time to deny this, to fill the void. An example will help to make clearer what she means by this. Suppose I give something to someone else—a gift, or some help, or whatever. What I cannot bear in such a situation, says Weil, is to receive *nothing* in return: thanks, a smile, a gesture, a gift later in return. Weil thinks of my need to receive something in return as a kind of mechanical need of the human soul—she calls it "gravity"—and as a craving for energy to help me go on. We are like machines that need such energy—whatever we give out to the world we want back from it in some form or other—and this *is* fleeing the unbearable void that *one is*, the void that I see I am when I realize I have a need for a return from the world in the kind of way indicated. In that moment, I grasp what I am, confront the reality of what I am. Our very being is, therefore, for Weil, a kind of sullying of the world, since we each live with the illusion that we *are* something and that we can *demand* something of the world, that is, just that return of energy. This demand is an imposing of oneself on the world that necessarily distorts (one's view of) it, since it presupposes, or expresses, the idea that I am at the center of the world, that I am something whose needs matter.

For this reason, Weil's ethical project is that of what she calls "decreation." "Once one has understood that one is nothing, the goal of all one's efforts is to become nothing," she said.[1] If I am utterly detached from all—*detachment* is another key term for Weil—then—and here we bring in the Christian context of Weil's thought—God will fill the void that I am. I am the void; I flee this all the time; if I cease, even for a moment, to flee it, I touch who, what, I really am; that is the void—but it is also God in the form of his grace that will fill the void. Ceasing to flee the void is nothing I can *do*, in a direct sense. All I can do is to turn away from evil, central to which is, we anticipate by now, my sense of myself as something. So, God does not love me. He can love himself through me insofar as I am "decreated." And he can love the world *through me* in the same way, which means, through my emptiness.

Now, I do not mean, of course, in saying that Berg-mann's project bears a similarity to that of Weil that he entertained any of the thoughts that Weil offers us. Obviously enough, I have no idea what was in his heart and mind as he prepared to erase his identity from the world. But Weil helps us see what the philosophical import is of what he did.

To wish to be nothing is a Christian desire. That is, more exactly, it is a desire that has been most clearly and profoundly developed and explored by Christianity, as in the case of Weil, even if exists at times wholly outside that conceptual, spiritual, and moral framework, and even if it is alien—as it is, as I pointed out in the introduction—to certain forms of Christianity. Christianity, as Weil understands it, takes Christ's life and teaching in as literal a way as possible, with his injunctions to us to love our enemies and pray for those who persecute us; to forgive unconditionally and limitlessly; to divest ourselves of worldly goods and shun social success; to love all equally, rejecting forms of love that single out some as more important to us than others; and so on. Christianity (in this sense) wishes to turn the world upside down—even if almost all Christians without exception have sought to convince themselves that they can live the Christian life whilst keeping the world the right way up. We are all more or less deeply attached to "worldliness—the love of pleasure, success, art, ourselves, and conversely, [are filled with] the fear of boredom, failure, being ridiculous, dying," as W. H. Auden put it, and most Christians are as much like that as the rest of us, even if they fool themselves into supposing they are not.[2] (Mrs. Bulstrode, remarks George Eliot in a magnificently icy observation in *Middlemarch*, believed in "the nothingness of this life and the desirability of cut glass.") But Weil really did want to live in a truly Christ-like spirit, rejecting as so much trash the things the rest of us care about. And it is as if the meaning of Peter Bergmann's life were that we can read from it the truth of such a vision of life: that what we all care for is, indeed, so much trash. He detaches himself utterly from the world, scorning that intense longing we all have to leave a trace, a mark of ourselves: a book, children, a family name, and the like. The act of his death as he stages it, his gesture of contempt for all that keeps the world going, is an act through which we can see a redemption of his self, of himself. In this sense, his emptying of himself is a gesture of rapture—not in the sense that he felt in such a state during that weekend in the hotel in Sligo, but in the sense that the image of the loss of self in this way is an image of liberation from the trammels of the self that weigh it down. We glimpse this freedom in the light cast by the deed of this utterly normal man staying in a hotel in Ireland. Perhaps Kierkegaard would have called him a knight of faith: the utterly unexceptional man the *spirit* of whose deed nonetheless is deep with wisdom and religious insight, even if his *mind* is not—and even if, perhaps especially if, he were the first to look baffled at someone who said this of him to him.

Here, as so often in human life, the view from the inside, so to speak, cannot tell us really what is going on. Virtually all that is good in human life is inextricably bound up with motives of greed, envy, pride, lust, and so on and would not be what it is without these. Philosophers have never really interested themselves in the fact that the virtues would be empty and barren without the vices, that the former need to be nourished by the latter, preferring to avert their eyes and suppose that there could be a wholly virtuous life with no admixture of the vices. They have therefore not explored the real issue, which is how to make sure that the vices do not get out of hand, supposing that the real problem is how to get rid of the vices altogether. But, as I say, it is important to get the right perspective. In Conrad's *The Nigger of the "Narcissus,"* he writes of the ship:

> She had her own future; she was alive with the lives of those beings who trod her decks; like that earth which had given her up to the sea, she had an intolerable load of regrets and hopes. On her lived timid truth and audacious lies; and, like the earth, she was unconscious, fair to see— and condemned by men to an ignoble fate. The august loneliness of her path lent dignity to the sordid inspiration of her pilgrimage.[3]

This utterly brilliant passage tells us where we have to look for anything redemptive in human affairs. Do not look, Conrad is telling us, at the inner working of minds and motives, for even in the very best of what human beings can produce—great music, paintings, poetry, scientific discovery—you will find that behind and beneath it there were shabby, second-rate motives at best. Not a single human being, including those who have produced that which redeems us from being an utterly grotesque species, can survive the glare inside if you are searching for purity of motive and desire. There can be dignity in a life—say, in its devotion to art or science—whose inner motivations would be dispiriting in the extreme to behold.

So Peter Bergmann's magnificent gesture of self-effacement is not magnificent because his motives were pure. They almost certainly were not. He was probably as shabby and second-rate as the rest of us. But the meaning of his gesture has a peculiar nobility about it, casting a light for us on the mediocrity of what we nearly always care about, even as we know it to be so much dross.

▶ ▷ ▶

It must be said, however, that Weil sought an emptying of the self *from the inside.* She really did want to empty herself of all the vices, and, to her credit, she saw that that would not leave the virtues intact but would destroy them altogether, leaving the self utterly empty. Her honesty from that point of view puts to shame what most philosophers say when they start to write and speak about morality. She wanted there to be no gap between her life and her thinking. She would have rejected wholly Conrad's view, saying that the smallest admixture of greed or envy or lust in one's motivations rendered worthless any achievement that they might otherwise have contributed to. Hence it is that she claims that you can read back from the purity of a work of art to the purity of the soul of the person who created it.

> It is true that talent has no connexion with morality; but then, there is no greatness about talent. It is untrue that there is no connexion between perfect beauty, perfect truth and perfect justice: they are far more than just connected: they form a single mysterious unity, for the good is one. . . . The *Iliad*, the tragedies of Aeschylus and those of Sophocles bear the clearest indication that the poets who produced them were in a state of holiness. . . . A tragedy like *King Lear* is the direct fruit of the pure spirit of love . . . Monteverdi, Bach, Mozart were beings whose lives were pure even as were their works.[4]

This, of course, is moralizing absurdity. We know perfectly well that Mozart and the rest were not pure as Weil claims they were. But when someone who is manifestly deeply sensitive and thoughtful says something so silly, we need to ask: Why? What is going on? Why would anyone want to say what Weil says? The answer is that she could not bear the ramshackle, compromised nature of the world, of the human soul in its relation to the world, and to itself. She could not bear to think that the greatest of human achievements come out of a psychological and cultural soil that was anything other than as great as those works themselves. And at the very least we can see that she is honest about what the problem is. In fact, her motivation here is little different from that of those—most—philosophers who claim, or hope, that virtue can get along without vice. The difference is that they suppose one could have all the good things—say, in art—without the vices that are needed to help produce them. Weil knows this to be humbug, so she denies that most art is any good anyway, and, where even she cannot dismiss a given work, as in the case of *King Lear*, she is forced to deny that Shakespeare was in anything other than a state of grace when he wrote it.

Weil, then, strove for a state of nothingness from the inside out. This is why she could say that "every time that I think of the crucifixion of Christ, I commit the sin of envy."[5] There is in this comment a kind of rapturous desperation to free herself entirely from the limits of the human. Weil wanted her own destruction, though her term for that was, as we have seen, "decreation." And what is striking is that this was not simply a spiritual destruction. Much has been written about her death at only thirty-four years of age and how to interpret it. What is certain is that, already extremely frail and, furthermore, ill with tuberculosis, she was instructed to rest and eat well. The maximum that she would allow herself to eat, however, was the quantity of food that her compatriots might have available to them in German-occupied France, an obvious gesture of solidarity. Some have claimed that she refused to eat in any case; others, that she could not eat even as she wanted to since she was so ill anyway. Either way, she did not eat enough and declined rapidly, dying of cardiac arrest.

I am not sure that the rather unseemly debate about whether Weil wanted to eat but could not, or refused to do so, is really to the point. Let us grant that she wanted to eat but could not. It seems to me nonetheless that her early death was what her whole life had been aiming at anyway: it was in many ways the fulfilment of its meaning. Her death as it occurred was entirely in keeping with her immense asceticism and self-punishing attitude. In that sense, her death suited her; whether she actually wanted to die there and then in that way is hardly to the point: it was the only reasonable outcome of her life as she had actually lived it, and she would have worked toward such a result in one way or another, come what may.

I do not at all wish to lose this created world from my view, but that it no longer be to me personally that it show itself. It cannot tell me its secret, for that is too high. If I go, then the creator and the creature will exchange their secrets.

To see a landscape as it is when I am not there . . .

When I am in any place, I sully the silence of heaven and earth by my breathing and the beating of my heart.[6]

Moreover, she thought of death as a purification—and her whole life was a longing for purity: "There are only two moments of perfect nudity and purity in human life: birth and death. It is only when we newly born or on our death-bed that we can adore God in human form without sully-ing the divinity."[7]

Although those who admire Weil like to distinguish sharply between her vocation to spiritual self-emptying and literal corporeal death, it is far from clear that things can be kept as tidy as that in this life that she longed so much to lead at the extreme. And from that point of view, her death and that of Bergmann are even more uncannily similar. Yet, in a certain way, his is more admirable. If you really think, as Weil said she did, that you disturb heaven and earth sim-ply by being alive, as you breathe and as your heart beats, what sense does it make to spend so much time leaving traces of oneself in the writing of books and essays? For sure, Weil kept much of her written material to herself, but she published a fair bit anyway, including late in life when she was developing the thinking that I have, in part, been pursuing here. Perhaps Weil was more than usually free of the greed, envy, and egoism that motivates writers. But even if this is so, they were sure to be there in her, and, anyway, to write and publish a book is to want to have some effect in the world, however minuscule in the scheme of things. It seems, if one may put it this way, much more of a distur-bance of heaven and earth than breathing is. It may seem unfair to say this, but I doubt that Weil should have written at all, except, perhaps, only and strictly for herself. None of those who admire her and write about her without criticiz-ing her—it is striking that much writing on her, including philosophical writing, is a form of hagiography—would even dream of trying to live as she did, as Susan Sontag pointed out. And they are right not to want to do so because, if they desire to write about her, they have to reject her sense of what it is to disturb heaven and earth. They do not, in my view, in their writings make it plain enough that they do, but their actions make the point. George Orwell, in an exceptionally acute discussion of Tolstoy's hatred of Shakespeare and his love of the world, makes a comment that is pertinent in this context:

> If only, Tolstoy says in effect, we would stop breeding, fighting, struggling and enjoying, if we could get rid not only of our sins but of everything else that binds us to the surface of the earth ... then the whole painful process would be over and the Kingdom of Heaven would arrive. But a normal human being does not want the Kingdom of Heaven: he wants life on earth to continue. This is not solely because he is "weak," "sinful" and anxious for a "good time." Most people get a fair amount of fun out of their lives, but on balance life is suffering, and only the very young or the very foolish imagine otherwise. Ultimately it is the Christian attitude which is self-interested and hedonistic, since the aim is always to get away from the painful struggle of earthly life and find eternal peace in some kind of Heaven or Nirvana. The humanist attitude is that the struggle must continue and that death is the price of life. "Men must endure their going hence, even as their coming hither: Ripeness is all"—which is an un-Christian sentiment. Often there is a seeming truce between the humanist and the religious believer, but in fact their attitudes cannot be reconciled: one must choose between this world and the next. And the enormous majority of human beings, if they

understood the issue, would choose this world. They do make that choice when they continue working, breeding and dying instead of crippling their faculties in the hope of obtaining a new lease of existence elsewhere.[8]

Now, Weil certainly did not hope for a lease of life elsewhere: she would have regarded that as just another expression of the miserable round of the ego from which Christian faith and life was supposed to free one. But why did she not see her writing in that way too? She crippled her faculties—to use Orwell's phrase—to get a new lease, or form, of existence *here*, but, though she liked to say that the ignorant peasant was wiser than Aristotle since the latter was so worldly—and he most certainly was—while the peasant in his simple dedication to his work was closer to God, she would not have dreamt of giving up her brilliant mind. She was utterly incapable of living quietly and leaving the world alone, despite the fact that her own thinking bade her do so. In her own way she was, as was Tolstoy, a spiritual bully.

Weil had, in other words, the usual problem that faces Christians: how to reconcile its desire to subvert all life that comes naturally to human beings with that life itself. For that subversion is, as I mentioned before, what Jesus demands when requiring of us total purity of thought, forgiveness of those who torment and torture us, love of enemies, perfect meekness, and so on. Weil was much more honest than most Christians in trying to live literally in accord with such ideals, for the overwhelming majority of whom, even the most admirable, being a Christian does not mean living a Christ-like life, and it is for this reason, above all others, that she is, in my view, admirable.

But, for all that, the quietism that her thinking expresses remained beyond her—and she could not live with that fact. So her path to self-destruction was clearly laid out. Peter Bergmann, for his part, spent a weekend cultivating his garden, so to speak: quietly going about his business, erasing himself with nothing showy or self-aggrandizing at all. This is why, I think, there is something moving in his example for the light it casts on our understanding of human life.

▶ ▷ ▶

I have long been fascinated by a fantasy of anonymity, of being somewhere where no one knows who I am or what I am doing there, of being hidden. Spending a night alone in a hotel where no one knows me and without those who know me knowing that this is where I am has always had a peculiar attraction for me. I like, too, leaving the house and walking a long distance on my own, leaving my whereabouts to friends and family unclear or vague. I am sure that this desire for anonymity is one reason that I like living abroad—I have lived in Germany, Austria, Italy, and Spain—since when I arrive my identity is empty for those around me—and thus for me. I find something liberating in anonymity. Not that I want to *do* anything in particular with this anonymity; I just wish to *be*. I wish to be as something unknown and something empty, evacuated; to enter, one might say, into a new epistemological and ontological relation to myself and others.

Given this peculiar quirk of my temperament, I do not think it is very surprising that the case of Peter Bergmann gripped me the moment I came across it. He lived out, as

it were, my fantasy. What he lived out for me was my desire
to free myself from myself, a sense of weariness with my
own personality. I imagine that everyone feels this from
time to time about him- or herself. It is just one aspect of
the way in which dissatisfaction is built into the human
condition, the way in which we live at odds with ourselves,
so often disappointed when we finally get what we want,
riven by conflicting desires, bored and overexcited by
turns, and so on. As Orwell said: "Most people get a fair
amount of fun out of their lives, but on balance life is suffering, and only the very young or the very foolish imagine
otherwise." Perhaps, then, the very fascination with the
Bergmann case lies most fundamentally for all of us in
this sense of freedom from the travails of the self. There is
something dignified in his calm resolve to erase himself.
In one of Willa Cather's short stories, "Consequences,"
two characters, Cavenaugh and Eastman, discuss someone called Wyatt who has committed suicide. Cavenaugh
comments: "He didn't leave any letters, either; people of
any taste don't. They wouldn't leave any material reminder
if they could help it."[9] From that point of view we might say
that Bergmann exhibited very refined taste. He knew when
he had had enough of himself and left with quiet dignity,
involving no one else. In a peculiar way the fact that he
killed himself in this way expresses a certain kind of fidel-
ity to the material world. It may be true, as Kant once
remarked in a discussion of suicide, that one can do so as
if one were leaving a smoke-filled room, but it would be a
mistake to think that all suicides are like this: the act can
be committed in a quite different spirit, a fact that Christianity has often wished to deny. It is possible to kill oneself
in part because one loves the world so much. I think of

Virginia Woolf's suicide in this way, for example. The note that she left for her husband was so full of love and gratitude that it would be impossible to think she left the world as if she were leaving a smoke-filled room: this disdain for things was nowhere in her heart.

In the film *The Last Days of Peter Bergmann*, directed by Ciaran Cassidy, on which I have drawn in this chapter, Detective Superintendent John Reilly, who led the investigation into the case, says that the images of Bergmann caught on CCTV as he walked around Sligo, disposing of his last possessions, have a haunting quality. He is certainly right, but I think he misidentifies why this is so. He seems to imply that it is the fact that Bergmann is always alone that gives the images this quality, but surely the real reason is that we know what happened shortly after the images were taken. To echo something that John Berger says about a painter and his or her paintings in his book on the doctor John Sassell: if I look at a photographic image of a person who, I know, is alive, I will see one thing; if I look at the image of someone who is dead, and I know this, I shall see something else.[10] A photograph of someone I see today, while he is still alive, is the same photograph as the photograph of him that I see tomorrow when he has died; but it is not the same image. I see, precisely, a dead man, and, in seeing this, I know that his life is now mine, not his. It is not continuing on in its mysterious struggles of love, hope, disappointment, fear, vulnerability, joy . . . with his trying to make sense of it all for himself. He has had his chance to make sense of it; that is now over. His life is now mine in that it is up to me—and anyone else who thinks of this man too, of course—to make sense of the life he led or make sense of the glimpses I get—as it might be, through precisely this photograph. The pictures of Bergmann caught on camera during his weekend in Sligo are what they are because by the Tuesday morning he was dead, and he had died in this very particular way. Had he not died, they would not be what they in fact are.

It may be that Reilly misidentifies the issue here because we all of us have a tendency to conflate and confuse being alone, being solitary, and being lonely. In truth, as we all know, it is possible to be lonely when talking and joking with others, just as one can be alone and not at all lonely. The fact that Bergmann was alone is, I think, neither here nor there from the point of view of his being lonely or otherwise. He may have been lonely, of course, but we cannot see that in the images. To think otherwise is to make an assumption—the assumption, indeed, that being alone means being lonely.

In any case, it is not true that Bergmann was wholly alone. I do not mean that he spoke to the staff at the hotel and so on, though he did that. It is rather that it is known that on the Saturday morning he went to the post office and bought eight 82-cent stamps and airmail stickers. Apparently, he sent some letters. But the investigation has never established to whom he wrote (assuming he did), where he posted the letters, or when he posted them. The people or person to whom he wrote were with him, in his mind and perhaps in his heart. Or it may be that he bought these stamps and stickers and then did nothing with them: he may easily have disposed of them with the rest of his possessions. Perhaps he was being mischievous in buying them, knowing that there would be a record of his having done so and wishing to muddy the waters, thinking of those who would try to make sense of his purchase. There could have been, for him, something really delicious in such a game. I like to think that his whole life had been lived under the sign of mischief. Perhaps it really was so.

7

Philippe Petit

A Life Lived in the Spirit of Rapture

To me it's really so simple that life should be lived on the
edge of life. You have to exercise rebellion. To refuse to
tape yourself to rules. To refuse your own success. To refuse
to repeat yourself. To see every day, every year, every idea as
a true challenge. And then you are going to live your life on
a tightrope.

So says the high-wire walker, juggler, pickpocket, magi-
cian, unicyclist, woodworker, horse rider, and writer
Philippe Petit. It would be hard, I think, to find a better
expression of the idea of a life lived in the spirit of rapture.

Petit is most famous for his wire walk on August 7,
1974, between the twin towers of the now destroyed World
Trade Center in New York, though this was only the most
spectacular of many such walks: between the towers of
Notre Dame; between the northern pylons of Sydney Har-
bour Bridge; high above the interior concourse of Grand
Central Terminal in New York; on an incline up to the
Eiffel Tower; and many more.

Petit is possessed, in his own words, of "an arrogant, proud and aggressive determination."[1] He is rebellious and says that all his ideas border on obsession. There is in him the spirit of the outlaw, the person who lives just within, and not infrequently beyond, the law. There is something of the criminal in him. Yet "the difference between a bank job and an illegal high-wire walk is paramount: the aerial crossing does not steal anything; it offers an ephemeral gift, one that delights and inspires." And he has "little respect for the established values of competition, money or social status."[2]

Petit tells us that, when he is performing, he is aware of the audience. Nonetheless:

> The true artistic impulse has nothing to do with pleasing the audience—or, for that matter, with pleasing the impresario so you'll get more jobs or money. That's not art. If you are an artist, you want to create a giant wall around yourself and, inside the wall, to follow your honesty and your intuition. What the audience will see is a man or woman who is prisoner of his or her passion, and that is the most inspiring performance in the world.[3]

Paul Auster, commenting on a performance of Petit's that he saw in Paris, writes:

> Unlike other street performers, he did not play to the crowd. Rather, it was as if he had allowed the audience to share in the workings of his thoughts, had made us privy to some deep, inarticulate obsession within him. Yet there was nothing overtly personal about what he did. Everything was revealed metaphorically, as if at one remove

through the medium of the performance. His juggling was precise and self-involved, like some conversation he was holding with himself. He elaborated the most complex combinations, intricate mathematical patterns, arabesques of nonsensical beauty, while at the same time keeping his gestures as simple as possible. Through it all, he managed to radiate a hypnotic charm, oscillating somewhere between demon and clown. No one said a word. It was as though his silence were a command for others to be silent as well. The crowd watched, and after the performance was over, everyone put money in the hat. I realized that I had never seen anything like it before.[4]

Petit shows us the shallowness of the distinction between the impersonal and the personal. One could say: it is almost misleading to say that Petit follows *his* passion. Or: *his* passion is an impersonal passion, not his at all. He is in the grip of something that exceeds him. "I am not *motivated* to do what I do. As an artist, I am driven, I am compelled, I am thrust forward by a force so rooted inside me, so convincing, that it seems futile to try to explain it. Although it has a name: passion."[5] Petit performs in obedience to his art. Even if no one else in the world obeyed in this way, even if no one else could understand his obedience and all looked askance at him, his performance would remain beyond both the personal and the impersonal. He says to us: the most deeply impersonal in human life is the most deeply personal. And the most deeply impersonal comes to the fore when someone stakes his all on something that *calls* him, that demands of *him* that he act in a certain way. When a man or woman is called by the deepest of passions, these passions show us the way in which our lives are not our own but lived out in accord with the demands of something impersonal in us. The young Törleß in Robert Musil's novel asks himself this: "Is it a general law that there is something in us that is stronger, greater, more beautiful, more passionate, darker than we are? Over which we have so little power that we can only aimlessly strew a thousand seeds until suddenly from one of them a seedling shoots like a dark flame that grows up far over us? ... And in every nerve of his body there trembled an impatient Yes in answer."[6] Petit answers in the same way. He loses himself to find himself, is always beyond himself, outside himself, which is a way of being deeply inside himself, alone. "In order to offer my most honest performance, I must be all alone. I must be prisoner of the fortress of my art."[7]

Petit does not tell us how to go about living our life. He tells us how he lives, and he hopes that we might "catch" something of that spirit and find a place for it in our life. In doing this, Petit offers us a vision of a kind of freedom. Freedom for him is an achievement. One is not free. One works toward one's freedom, and each day it needs to be reconquered, acquired anew.

If one is to catch something of Petit's spirit, how does this happen? Obviously enough, it is not a matter of becoming a high-wire walker! Yet many of those who come into contact with him—be it personally, as in the case of Auster, or through his performances, interviews and books—have a sense of being enriched by the contact, a deepened sense of the possibilities of life.

Certain aspects of this come out, I think, in the film *Man on Wire* (2008), directed by James Marsh, from which I took Petit's comments at the outset of this chapter. Petit's girlfriend at the time, Annie Allix, for example, says that, when she met him, through being bound up "in his life I completely forget my own. And he did not bother to find out if I had a path to follow. It was obvious that I had to follow his path." The significance of this comes out most fully when she says that, after his walk between the twin towers, their love story was at an end. She says that she found this fitting. It is clear that she saw her life as being immeasurably enriched by being consumed in his project. The same comes out with his friend, the photographer Jean-Louis Blondeau, one of his accomplices on the walk, when Blondeau remarks, very movingly, that there was something broken in his friendship with Petit after the walk—and then he is overcome with tears at the sense of what they had achieved together and of its significance. It is clear that these two—and certainly others who were involved as well—experienced the whole thing as a gift, as if they were caught up in the overflowing, overwhelming energy of it all.

But most people's contact with Petit is, of course, through his performances. About these, Auster says this:

> Working under the greatest possible constraints, on a stage no more than an inch wide, the high-wire walker's job is to create a sensation of limitless freedom. Juggler, dancer, acrobat, he performs in the sky what other men are content to perform on the ground. The desire is at once far-fetched and perfectly natural, and the appeal of it, finally, is its utter uselessness. No art, it seems to me, so clearly emphasizes the deep aesthetic impulse in all of us. Each time we see a man walk on the wire, a part of us is up there with him. Unlike performances in the other arts, the

experience of the high wire is direct, unmediated, simple, and it requires no explanation whatsoever. The art is the thing itself, a life in its most naked delineation. And if there is beauty in this, it is because of the beauty we feel inside ourselves.[8]

Later he says: "High-wire walking is not an art of death but an art of life—and life lived to the very extreme of life. Which is to say, life that does not hide from death, but stares it directly in the face." And because it is this, it is a way of testing oneself to the limit: "The high-wire is an art of solitude, a way of coming to grips with one's life in the darkest, most secret corner of the self."[9]

I think that Auster captures well the sense of something breathtakingly moving in Petit's wire walking, the feeling that he pushes at the limits of the human, transcends himself, and yet is returned to himself. And there is without doubt an incredible beauty in his walks, in this sense that one is seeing someone floating in the sky, high-up there, a speck against the heavens. The human being here is tiny and yet, in the achievement, possesses an immense grandeur. One aspect of that grandeur is that we sense in Petit someone who has an immense hunger for life. Most of us find, I think, that we get sadder as we get older, and with the sadness often comes a sense of fatigue and a longing to experience again the rapturous moments of existence that were ours when we were young and insouciant. Petit seems untouched by that fatigue, and he certainly lives with what Nietzsche called an "overflowing, generous, squandering spirit." Nietzsche despised those who live constantly, as it were, on the lookout for their own benefit, for "getting on," always anxious about what they possess or can acquire. In some ways, he hated this so much because his ill-health forced him to spend much more time than he liked in an anxious, self-enclosed preoccupation with his own state, and he despised himself for it. He longed for the release that someone like Petit embodies. But one does not have to be as anxiously self-concerned as Nietzsche was to appreciate the force of Petit's example, and I think philosophers have been far too inattentive to the ways in which we need contact with specific others to find our bearings in life. Most moral philosophy, for example, deals in abstract discussion of virtue, duty, welfare, and so on, with little serious attention to how these are embodied in individual lives: philosophers' examples of individuals tend to be schematic at best. But, more important, it is not simply a question here of the fact that to make sense of, say, the virtues, we need to see them embodied in specific lives; it is also that we need *contact* with the individuals who embody them if we are to find a way to make space for them in our life. I need to be in the *presence* of others to grasp what the possibilities are for my life, and I intend that at least in part not as a comment on something we need instead of philosophy, but as a complement to it. And that presence may be through personal encounter or something else—reading of others' lives, seeing a film about them, hearing a talk they give, or watching, as it may be, a high-wire walk. Auster is right that the utter uselessness of what Petit does is precisely its point: as Schiller remarked, we are only truly human when we play. Petit's play on the high-wire, or, more exactly, his play, one expression of which is the high-wire, inspires us because it nourishes our sense of why life is worth living. Petit *reminds* us that life is worth living. But being told that life is worth

139

living is really beside the point. We need to *see* it in someone—and we see it deeply and in an exemplary fashion in Petit. What he does is nothing but entertainment. And precisely because it is nothing but entertainment— entertainment of the first rank, of course—it is of irreplaceable importance in life. If life is tragic, this means that we have need of figures like Petit, not to conceal the truth from us, nor yet to act as a kind of "compensation" to keep us going, as it were, but to show us that joy, delight, fun, and entertainment, when taken to the kinds of rapturous limits we see in his life, go as deep with human beings as does tragedy. Rapture, I am saying, is as profound as tragedy in human life. But we miss this because tragedy more readily comes to us than does rapture. Tragedy stalks every human life in one way or another, but rapture has to be cultivated. By this I do not mean that one needs to go in search of rapture; that would only make it all the more elusive. I mean that one needs to cultivate an openness to rapture, to receiving it when it comes along, as it were by chance, and this may require, as in the case of Petit, hard work: "No, the high wire is not what you think it is. It is not a realm of lightness, space, and smiles. It is a job. Grim, tough, deceptive."[10] You can make of your life a tragedy by aiming to do so: nothing is easier for human beings than to be destructive, for nothing comes more easily to human beings than negative energy. But you cannot aim to fill your life with rapture. What you can do is seek to fill your life with things that grip you, transport you, take you to the edge of life. You can, as Petit says, listen to the rebellious voice in you, and this will *be* a life lived in a spirit of rapture and may well contain moments of rapture. But most of us are too indolent, too in love with ourselves and our own ease and comfort, to bother. And we know this. This is why Petit inspires us—because he also puts us to shame, makes us face our own lethargy and complacency.

▶ ▷ ▶

Petit says: "To put your whole foot on the wire all at once produces a sure though heavy kind of walking, but if you first slide your toes, then your sole, and finally your heel onto the wire, you will be able to experience the intoxicating lightness that is so magnificent at great heights."[11] Reflecting on philosophy, metaphysics, and the soul, Michel Serres says that the gymnast's soul is found at the point where his or her body curls around or seeks out or comes into contact with the apparatus used: the fixed bar, somersault rings, the floor, the trampoline. In football, the players' soul is out there, in the ball. So we can say: Petit's soul is in his feet. And he wishes to treat his soul with great delicacy, tenderness: hence his comments about how to walk across the wire.

"Jumping," says Serres, "constitutes the second bodily pleasure after breathing."[12] This is because it is *flight*, and he speaks of running, not as accelerated walking, but as a kind of generalized jumping. He adores those merry-go-rounds with small seats suspended on chains, each one of which carries a single person. Flight again. A pole-vaulter earns his undying admiration. And then the trampoline: "Does there exist on the earth any object more marvellous than the trampoline, has human technology ever invented a device more divine?"[13] Well, perhaps. Perhaps it is the high wire. Here, surely, is flight. Petit flies on his feet. I am sure that Serres would agree.

You who profess to speak—professors, actors, solicitors, all kinds of rhetors—you whose daily activity uses song, who must make your voice carry outside your body to fill a space stretching as far as the back wall and who have to lift a vibrating column, concentrated sounds and exquisite inflections, like a whirlpool of fire above your throat, be aware that everything comes from your base, positioning and posture on the earth, from your balance, from your instinctive gripping of the ground with the soles of your feet, from your grasping hold of long roots with your toes.[14]

So says Serres. We can say: in making us think so intensely of the feet, Petit tells us the same thing. He says: you who deal in words owe me everything. I tell you what you are. You are feet that speak, and you know this because I am feet that speak, I am feet that speak because they are silent, because they do everything. My feet root me to the ground and my feet make me fly. Your feet root you to the ground, but you need a voice, a voice that borrows its life from the feet. My feet lend nothing; they give freely, and what they give is the gift you receive when you watch me walking on the high wire. You, in the arrogance of your words that claim to know, know nothing of true arrogance, which is mine, superior to yours in every way.

This is why when—in an interview on the BBC Radio 4 program *Desert Island Discs*, in which guests speak about their life and choose eight pieces of music they would take with them to a desert island—Petit was given, as all guests are, the Bible and the complete works of Shakespeare, he said he would use the Bible as a stool to look at the horizon and watch for boats and the pages of Shakespeare to light his fire. He says: do not forget that Shakespeare has feet, and I tell him what he really is. The thought is, of course, mad, absurd, and yet, in a way, profoundly right, for in its mad presumption and arrogance it is central to Petit's life lived in the spirit of rapture.

► ▷ ►

Jean Genet wrote a short essay entitled "Le funambule," an act of homage to his then lover, the German-Algerian high-wire walker Abdallah Bentaga. At one point he writes:

> I know objects, their deviousness [*malignité*], their cruelty, also their gratitude. The wire was dead—or, if you wish, dumb, blind—and here you are: it will live and speak.
>
> You will love it, and with an almost carnal love. Every morning, and before starting your practice, when it is tense and vibrates, go and kiss it. Ask it to support you and to give you the elegance and edginess [*nervosité*] of the back of the knee. At the end of the performance, salute it, give it thanks. When it is coiled up in its box, at night, go and see it, caress it. And gently place your cheek against its cheek.[15]

143

The incantatory, lyrical style of Genet's writing here is typical of his work, and he evokes with it the intense complicity the wire walker has with his wire, his intense love and respect for it. For the walker has to know the wire through and through and to treat it with the utmost respect. Any mistake in this regard could mean a fall and death. Petit makes the same thing clear in his exploration of acquiring knowledge of ropes and preparing them for a walk:

The number of ropes . . . is infinite.

Whoever intends to master the art of walking on them must take on the task of seeking them out. Of comparing them. Of keeping those whose properties correspond to his aspirations. Of learning how to know them. Of knowing how to tighten them.

Acquiring this knowledge is the work of a lifetime.[16]

Genet goes so far as to say that it is the rope or wire that becomes the object of the spectacle, not the walker.

You will carry out your leaps, your jumps, your dances . . . not so that you shine but so that the wire of steel, which was dead and voiceless, might sing. How it will be grateful to you if your attitude towards it is perfect, not for your glory but for that of the wire.

The amazed audience will cry: "What an amazing wire! How it holds the dancer up and loves him!"[17]

Petit too speaks of the "song of the cable."[18] Vanishingly few of us know the material world as Petit does, his general knowledge here compressed into his knowledge of the wire, of wires. Virtually all of us live so far from the material things that surround us: they are *over there*, to be manipulated and used or avoided if dangerous or noxious. But Petit lives with them as, once, did carpenters and wheelwrights and blacksmiths and joiners and potters. Some, a few, in the modern world are discovering our intense loss and impoverishment here, our alienation from material things, our shallowness in relation to them. Petit shows us how we can have a rapturous relation to them and, once again, shames us, because he shows us what that costs in terms of dedication, effort, time, energy. Most of are unwilling even to think about expending ourselves in this way.

Petit is at one with the wire and with himself as the animals are at one with themselves and their material world. On the wire, he crosses as does a squirrel or monkey. The animals are not mind and body: they are at one with themselves, animated, living, vibrant bodies. This is what Petit is when he crosses the wire. He becomes wholly animal, his body completely at one with his mind. And both are at one with the wire. This is why Petit says: "Walking is the soul of the wire." And: "You will become wire."[19] The high-wire walker expresses an ideal for human beings—both beyond the human and yet beneath it as animal, and wholly at one with the material world.

In Petit we glimpse what it is truly to live. And if we can catch something of his spirit in our life, we shall be immeasurably enriched.

Acknowledgments

I should like to thank Costica Bradatan for inviting me to write a book in this series and for being so enthusiastic about my writing on the theme of rapture.

I am very grateful to Wendy Lochner and Lowell Frye at Columbia University Press for their support, advice, patience, and enthusiasm.

I should also like to thank two reviewers for Columbia University Press who kindly read an earlier version of this book. Both were extremely generous in their attention to my work and offered judicious criticisms as well as much encouragement. I have done my best to respond to their criticisms, but am acutely aware that I have not been able to do so as fully as I would have liked. All the inevitable faults of this work remain, therefore, my responsibility alone.

My greatest debt is, once again, to Nelly.

Notes

Introduction

1. Virginia Woolf, "Sketch of the Past," in *Moments of Being: Autobiographical Writings*, ed. Jeanne Schulkind, intro. Hermione Lee (London: Pimlico, 2002 [1940]), 84.
2. Woolf, 85.
3. Christopher Ricks, *Keats and Embarrassment* (Oxford: Oxford University Press, 1976), 97.
4. Bernard Williams, "*The Women of Trachis*: Fictions, Pessimism, Ethics," in *The Greeks and Us: Essays in Honor of W. H. Adkins*, ed. Robert B. Louden and Paul Schollmeier (Chicago: University of Chicago Press, 1996), 52.
5. Bertrand Russell, *Unpopular Essays* (London: George Allen, 1950), 64.
6. Tony Tanner, *Conrad: "Lord Jim"* (London: Edward Arnold, 1969), 57.

1. Nietzsche

1. Friedrich Nietzsche, *Die fröhliche Wissenschaft*, in *Sämtliche Werke: Kritische Studienausgabe*, ed. G. Colli and M. Montinari, 15 vols., Band 3, 2nd ed. (Berlin: Deutscher Taschenbuch Verlag, 1988 [1882–87]), 351.

1. NIETZSCHE

2. Maurice Merleau-Ponty, *The Visible and the Invisible*, ed. Claude Lefort, tr. Alphonso Lingis (Evanston, IL: Northwestern University Press, 1968 [1964]), 136–37, 139.

3. Friedrich Nietzsche, *Menschliches Allzumenschliches*, in *Sämtliche Werke: Kritische Studienausgabe*, ed. G. Colli and M. Montinari, 15 vols., Band 2, 2nd ed. (Berlin: Deutscher Taschenbuch Verlag, 1988 [1878–80]), 542.

4. Friedrich Nietzsche, *Ecce Homo*, in *Sämtliche Werke: Kritische Studienausgabe*, ed. G. Colli and M. Montinari, 15 vols., Band 6, 2nd ed. (Berlin: Deutscher Taschenbuch Verlag, 1988 [1908]), 295.

5. Friedrich Nietzsche, *Also sprach Zarathustra*, in *Sämtliche Werke: Kritische Studienausgabe*, ed. G. Colli and M. Montinari, 15 vols., Band 4, 2nd ed. (Berlin: Deutscher Taschenbuch Verlag, 1988 [1883–85]), 344.

6. Friedrich Nietzsche, *Morgenröte*, in *Sämtliche Werke: Kritische Studienausgabe*, ed. G. Colli and M. Montinari, 15 vols., Band 3, 2nd ed. (Berlin: Deutscher Taschenbuch Verlag, 1988 [1881]), 323.

7. Virginia Woolf, "On Being Ill," in *Selected Essays*, ed. David Bradshaw (Oxford: Oxford University Press, 2008 [1926]), 104–5.

8. Woolf, 106.

9. Nietzsche, *Die fröhliche Wissenschaft*, 349.

10. Stefan Zweig, *Der Kampf mit dem Dämon*, chap. 31, "Apologie der Krankheit," 1925, *Projekt Gutenberg*, https://www.projekt-gutenberg.org/zweig/kampfdae/kampfdae.html.

11. E. M. Cioran, *A Short History of Decay*, tr. Richard Howard (New York: Arcade, 1998 [1949]), 47–48.

3. Pierre Bonnard

1. Michel Serres, *The Five Senses: A Philosophy of Mingled Bodies*, intro. Steven Connor, tr. Margaret Sankey and Peter Cowley (London: Continuum, 2008 [1985]), 29–30.

2. John Berger, "Bonnard," in *The Sense of Sight*, ed. and intro. Lloyd Spencer (New York: Vintage International, 1985 [1969]), 92, 97.

3. Berger, 93.

4. Berger, 97.

5. Stendhal, *De l'amour*, biographical background and preface Michel Crouzet (Paris: Flammarion, 2011 [1822]), 34–35.

6. Berger, "Bonnard," 95.
7. Maurice Merleau-Ponty, *The Phenomenology of Perception*, tr. Colin Smith (London: Routledge, 2002 [1945]), 178.
8. Merleau-Ponty, 195–96.
9. Stefan Zweig, *Montaigne*, chap. 1, 1941/42, Projekt Gutenberg, https://www.projekt-gutenberg.org/zweig/schrifts/chap012.html.
10. Joseph Conrad, *Lord Jim*, chap. 23, 1899/1900, Project Gutenberg, https://www.gutenberg.org/files/5658/5658-h/5658-h.htm.
11. Zweig, *Montaigne*, chap. 1.

4. Reverie

1. Jean-Jacques Rousseau, *Les rêveries d'un promeneur solitaire*, intro. Érik Leborgne (Paris: Flammarion, 2012 [1782]), 95.
2. Rousseau, 102.
3. Rousseau, 103.
4. Robert P. Harrison, *Gardens: An Essay on the Human Condition* (Chicago: University of Chicago Press, 2008), ix.
5. Harrison, xii.
6. Rousseau, *Les rêveries d'un promeneur solitaire*, 103.
7. Virginia Woolf, *The Waves*, ed. and intro. Kate Flint (Harmondsworth: Penguin, 1992 [1931], 7.
8. Woolf, 18.
9. Woolf, 188.
10. W. H. Auden, "A Consciousness of Reality," in *Forewords and Afterwords*, selected by Edward Mendelson (New York: Vintage, 1989 [1954]), 414–15.
11. Alphonso Lingis, *Dangerous Emotions* (Berkeley: University of California Press, 2000), 105–6.
12. George Orwell, "Lear, Tolstoy and the Fool," in *The Penguin Essays of George Orwell* (Harmondsworth: Penguin, 1984 [1947]), 419.
13. John Berger, *and our faces, my heart, brief as photos* (London: Bloomsbury, 2005 [1984]), 101.
14. David E. Cooper, *A Philosophy of Gardens* (Oxford: Oxford University Press, 2008), 90–96.

5. The Kiss

1. Anton Chekhov, "The Kiss," in *The Kiss and Other Stories*, tr. and intro. Ronald Wilkes (Harmondsworth: Penguin, 1982 [1887]), 37.
2. Chekhov, 37–38.
3. Christopher Ricks, *Keats and Embarrassment* (Oxford: Oxford University Press, 1976), 99.
4. Émile Zola, *Thérèse Raquin*, chap. 21, 1868, *Project Gutenberg*, https://www.gutenberg.org/files/7461/7461-8.txt.

6. Nothingness

1. Simone Weil, *La pesanteur et la grâce* (Paris: Plon, 1991 [1947]), 84.
2. W. H. Auden, *Lectures on Shakespeare*, ed. Arthur C. Kirsch (Princeton, NJ: Princeton University Press, 2000), 365.
3. Joseph Conrad, *The Nigger of the "Narcissus,"* ed. Robert Kimbrough (New York: Norton, 1979 [1898]), 18.
4. Simone Weil, *The Need for Roots: Prelude to a Declaration of Duties Towards Mankind*, preface T. S. Eliot, tr. Arthur Mills (London: Routledge, 2001 [1949]), 229.
5. Simone Weil, *Waiting on God*, tr. Emma Craufurd (London: Routledge, 1977 [1950]), 36.
6. Weil, *La pesanteur et la grâce*, 37.
7. Weil, 88.
8. George Orwell, "Lear, Tolstoy and the Fool," in *The Penguin Essays of George Orwell* (Harmondsworth: Penguin, 1984 [1947]), 418.
9. Willa Cather, "Consequences," in *The Short Stories of Will Cather*, selected and intro. Hermione Lee (London: Virago, 2006 [1915]), 181.
10. John Berger and Jean Mohr, *A Fortunate Man: The Story of a Country Doctor*, intro. Gavin Francis (Edinburgh: Canongate, 2015 [1967]), 160–61.

7. Phillipe Petit

1. Philippe Petit, *Creativity* (New York: Riverhead, 2015), 2.
2. Petit, 3, 4.

3. Petit, 16.
4. Philippe Petit, *On the High Wire*, tr. and intro. Paul Auster (London: Weidenfeld and Nicolson, 1988), x–xi.
5. Petit, *Creativity*, 15.
6. Robert Musil, *Die Verwirrungen des Zöglings Törleß* (Hamburg: Rowohlt, 1991 [1906]), 92.
7. Petit, *Creativity*, 15.
8. Petit, *On the High Wire*, xiv–xv.
9. Petit, xxv, xxi.
10. Petit, 5.
11. Petit, 16.
12. Michel Serres, *The Five Senses: A Philosophy of Mingled Bodies*, intro. Steven Connor, tr. Margaret Sankey and Peter Cowley (London: Continuum, 2008 [1985]), 314.
13. Serres, 316.
14. Serres, 315–16.
15. Jean Genet, *Le funambule* (Paris: L'Arbalète Gallimard, 2010 [1958]), 9–10.
16. Petit, *On the High Wire*, 6–7.
17. Genet, *Le funambule*, 11.
18. Petit, *On the High Wire*, 12.
19. Petit, 16, 23.

Bibliography

Auden, W. H. "A Consciousness of Reality." In *Forewords and Afterwords.* Selected by Edward Mendelson, 411–18. New York: Vintage, 1989 [1954].

——. *Lectures on Shakespeare.* Ed. Arthur C. Kirsch. Princeton, NJ: Princeton University Press, 2000. (The lectures were originally given in 1946–47 at the New School in New York.)

Berger, John. "Bonnard." In *The Sense of Sight.* Ed. and intro. Lloyd Spencer, 92–98. New York: Vintage International, 1985 [1969].

——. *and our faces, my heart, brief as photos.* London: Bloomsbury, 2005 [1984].

Berger, John, and Jean Mohr. *A Fortunate Man: The Story of a Country Doctor.* Intro. Gavin Francis. Edinburgh: Canongate, 2015 [1967].

Cassidy, Ciaran. *The Last Days of Peter Bergmann.* Aeon Video. https://vimeo .com/166977498.

Cather, Willa. "Consequences." In *The Short Stories of Will Cather.* Selected and intro. Hermione Lee, 170–91. London: Virago, 2006 [1915].

Chekhov, Anton, "The Kiss." In *The Kiss and Other Stories.* Tr. and intro. Ronald Wilkes, 31–48. Harmondsworth: Penguin, 1982 [1887].

Cioran, E. M. *A Short History of Decay.* Tr. Richard Howard. New York: Arcade, 1998 [1949].

Conrad, Joseph. *Lord Jim.* 1899/1900. *Project Gutenberg.* https://www .gutenberg.org/files/5658/5658-h/5658-h.htm.

——. *The Nigger of the "Narcissus."* Ed. Robert Kimbrough. New York: Norton, 1979 [1898].

BIBLIOGRAPHY

Cooper, David E. *A Philosophy of Gardens*. Oxford: Oxford University Press, 2008.

Genet, Jean. *Le funambule*. Paris: L'Arbalète Gallimard, 2010 [1958].

Harrison, Robert P. *Gardens: An Essay on the Human Condition*. Chicago: University of Chicago Press, 2008.

Lingis, Alphonso. *Dangerous Emotions*. Berkeley: University of California Press, 2000.

Merleau-Ponty, Maurice. *The Visible and the Invisible*. Ed. Claude Lefort, tr. Alphonso Lingis. Evanston, IL: Northwestern University Press, 1968 [1964].

Merleau-Ponty, Maurice. *The Phenomenology of Perception*. Tr. Colin Smith. London: Routledge, 2002 [1945].

Musil, Robert. *Die Verwirrungen des Zöglings Törleß*. Hamburg: Rowohlt, 1991 [1906].

Nietzsche, Friedrich. *Also sprach Zarathustra*. In *Sämtliche Werke: Kritische Studienausgabe*. Ed. G. Colli and M. Montinari. 15 vols., Band 4, 2nd ed. Berlin: Deutscher Taschenbuch Verlag, 1988 [1883–85].

——. *Die fröhliche Wissenschaft*. In *Sämtliche Werke: Kritische Studienausgabe*. Ed. G. Colli and M. Montinari. 15 vols., Band 3, 2nd ed. Berlin: Deutscher Taschenbuch Verlag, 1988 [1882–86].

——. *Ecce Homo*. In *Sämtliche Werke: Kritische Studienausgabe*. Ed. G. Colli and M. Montinari. 15 vols., Band 6, 2nd ed. Berlin: Deutscher Taschenbuch Verlag, 1988 [1908].

——. *Menschliches Allzumenschliches*. In *Sämtliche Werke: Kritische Studienausgabe*. Ed. G. Colli and M. Montinari. 15 vols., Band 2, 2nd ed. Berlin: Deutscher Taschenbuch Verlag, 1988 [1878–80].

——. *Morgenröte*. In *Sämtliche Werke: Kritische Studienausgabe*. Ed. G. Colli and M. Montinari. 15 vols., Band 3, 2nd ed. Berlin: Deutscher Taschenbuch Verlag, 1988 [1881].

Orwell, George. "Lear, Tolstoy and the Fool." In *The Penguin Essays of George Orwell*, 407–22. Harmondsworth: Penguin, 1984 [1947].

Petit, Philippe. *Creativity*. New York: Riverhead, 2015.

——. *On the High Wire*. Tr. and intro. Paul Auster. London: Weidenfeld and Nicolson, 1988.

Ricks, Christopher. *Keats and Embarrassment*. Oxford: Oxford University Press, 1976.

BIBLIOGRAPHY

Rousseau, Jean-Jacques. *Les rêveries d'un promeneur solitaire*. Intro. Érik Leborgne. Paris: Flammarion, 2012 [1782].

Russell, Bertrand. *Unpopular Essays*. London: George Allen, 1950.

Serres, Michel. *The Five Senses: A Philosophy of Mingled Bodies*. Intro. Steven Connor, tr. Margaret Sankey and Peter Cowley. London: Continuum, 2008 [1985].

Stendhal. *De l'amour*. Biographical background and preface Michel Crouzet. Paris: Flammarion, 2011 [1822].

Tanner, Tony. *Conrad: "Lord Jim."* London: Edward Arnold, 1969.

Weil, Simone. *La pesanteur et la grâce*. Paris: Plon, 1991 [1947].

——. *The Need for Roots: Prelude to a Declaration of Duties Towards Mankind*. Preface T. S. Eliot, tr. Arthur Mills. London: Routledge, 2001 [1949].

——. *Waiting on God*. Tr. Emma Craufurd. London: Routledge, 1977 [1950].

Williams, Bernard. "*The Women of Trachis*: Fictions, Pessimism, Ethics." In *The Greeks and Us: Essays in Honor of W. H. Adkins*. Ed. Robert B. Louden and Paul Schollmeier, 43–53. Chicago: University of Chicago Press, 1996.

Woolf, Virginia. "On Being Ill." In *Selected Essays*. Ed. and intro. David Bradshaw, 101–10. Oxford: Oxford University Press, 2008 [1926].

——. "Sketch of the Past." In *Moments of Being: Autobiographical Writings*. Ed. Jeanne Schulkind, intro. Hermione Lee, 78–160. London: Pimlico, 2002 [1940].

——. *The Waves*. Ed. and intro. Kate Flint. Harmondsworth: Penguin, 1992 [1931].

Zola, Émile. *Thérèse Raquin*, Project Gutenberg. 1868. https://www.gutenberg .org/files/7461/7461-8.txt.

Zweig, Stefan. *Der Kampf mit dem Dämon*. 1925. Projekt Gutenberg. https:// www.projekt-gutenberg.org/zweig/kampfdae/kampfdae.html.

——. *Montaigne*. 1941/42. Projekt Gutenberg. https://www.projekt-gutenberg .org/zweig/schrifts/chap012.html.

Index

INDEX

Printed in the USA
CPSIA information can be obtained
at www.ICGtesting.com
LVHW041914070224
771043LV00001B/2